AF375216

Library of Congress Control Number: 2024918894
ISBN: 9798991251419

First Edition: 2024

CONTENTS

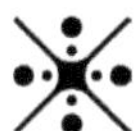

I sincerely thank my professors, Kyna Leski, Hansy Better, Carl Lostritto, Christopher Bardt, and Daniel Lefcourt. Your introductions to the beautiful world of art and design have enlightened me with wisdom and inspired my creative journey.

To my professional mentors, Mitchell Joachim and Vivian Kuan, your guidance has been invaluable. You have not only supported my professional growth but also encouraged me to pursue design leadership with passion and dedication.

To my friends who have helped and inspired me along my life journey, your influence has been deeply felt.

Finally, to my husband, Sebastian, and my wonderful family, your unwavering support has been the cornerstone of my ability to complete this book. Thank you for being my rock and a constant source of encouragement.

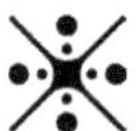

I want to express my deepest gratitude to everyone who has sparked my creativity and lent their support, and to those around me who have always believed in me.

Without you, I wouldn't be where I am today.

You have illuminated my life, and I aspire to bring the same light to others through love and art.

Special Acknowledgement for Land of Medicine Buddha

During the completion of this book, I had the honor of being invited to the Land of Medicine Buddha in Santa Cruz to exhibit and perform my multisensory art for meditation. The opportunity to collaborate with such a sacred place was both a rare and profound experience for me, validating the spiritual dimensions I explore in my work.

I extend my heartfelt gratitude to the Land of Medicine Buddha for their generous support and for granting me the chance to present my work in such a holy space. This extraordinary experience deeply moved me and became a significant milestone in my artistic journey. Creating and exhibiting my work in such a sacred environment was an immense honor and inspiration. Your trust and support not only deepened my understanding of the connection between art and the spiritual world but also allowed me to feel the immense power of creating within this sacred space.

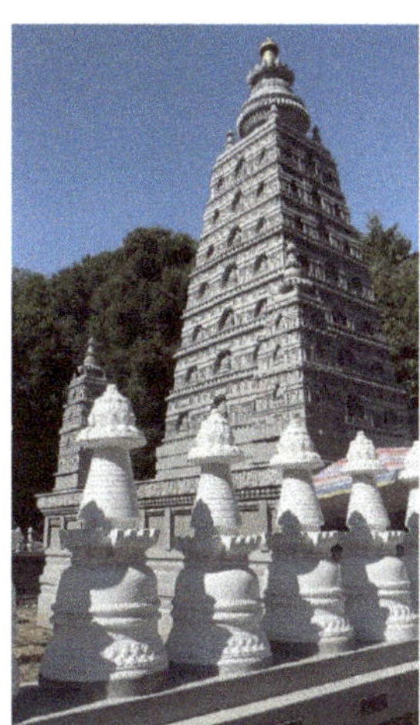 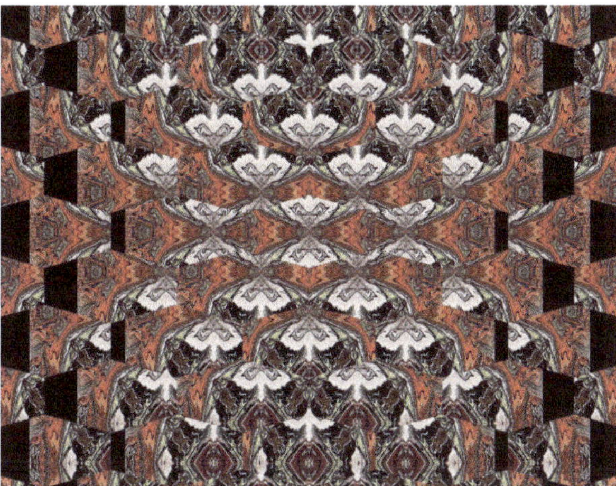

Kaleidoscopic Meditation - Land of Medicine Buddha Special Edition

While I have always understood the profound relationship between artwork, environment, people, and events, this was the first time I so intensely felt the energy and magnetic fields that a piece can generate in a specific setting.

On my way back, I dreamt that I had transformed into a raindrop, sliding off the eaves and falling into a pond filled with blooming lotuses. This dream felt like a revelation, guiding me to see my mission as an artist more clearly.

Through this book, I hope to convey this sacred feeling to every reader, to connect with more people through my art, and to soothe hearts through my creations.

8/23/2024

ABOUT THE AUTHOR

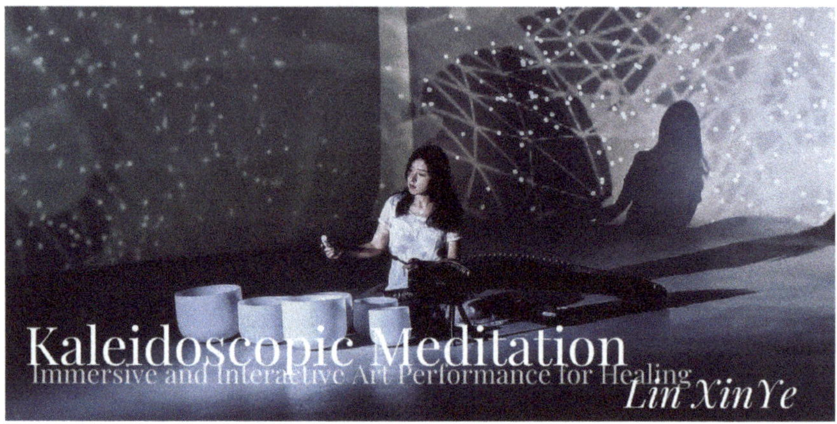

Xinye Lin is an award-winning multidimensional artist and designer who bridges hyper-traditional concepts with hyper-contemporary techniques. She graduated from the Rhode Island School of Design with a Master's in Architecture and holds a Bachelor's in Urban Planning. Her strong academic background supports her multimedia art and parametric design.

By integrating Eastern philosophy, advanced soft/hardware technologies, Chinese culture, the concepts of Wuxing and Yinyang, twenty-seven years of Guzheng experience, chanting, and personal meditation practices, her work creates immersive multisensory spaces that rejuvenate the mind, body, and soul. Xinye's art creations combine visual, auditory, olfactory, and tactile elements, exploring multisensory experiences and deeply delving into the intrinsic emotional connections among space, time, and people.

Xinye's works have been exhibited globally, including at Times Square in New York, the United Nations, the CHSA Museum, the Cooper Hewitt Design Museum, the CICA Museum, the Hong Kong Biennale, as well as at international art festivals such as Boston ILLUMINUS and Digital Graffiti in Florida. She has received accolades from numerous institutions, such as the United Nations Economic and Social Council, RISD Alumni Magazine, and www.artjobs.com etc.

Her artistic journey has spanned five continents and twenty-five countries, with each trip infusing new vitality and a deeper understanding of multiculturalism into her work. Her education and life experiences in Eastern and Western cultures provide rich material for her creations, allowing her to deeply appreciate cultural diversity and the boundless possibilities of artistic expression.

As an Asian female artist, Xinye has faced numerous challenges throughout her growth. She understands that everyone experiences different pain and hardship in their journey. Her mission is to transform these emotions into something beautiful and powerful. Xinye's art focuses on spiritual exploration, providing solace to the soul, conveying love and hope, and inspiring and touching the heart of every viewer.

www.linxinye.com
Scan to learn more

1

INTRODUCTION AND MY STORY

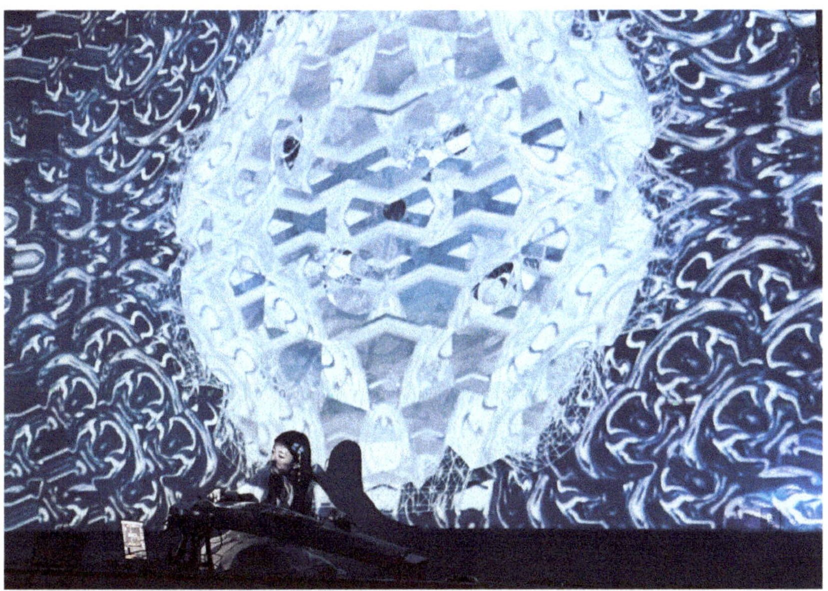

Floating Dream -Live Immersive & Interactive Art Performance and Solo Exhibition, San Francisco, 2023

Dear Reader,

Welcome to my world. I am Xinye Lin, an artist who has dedicated many years to exploring multisensory art and meditation.

In this book, I will take you on an unprecedented journey through art and meditation. By engaging your senses through color, sound, scent, touch, feng shui, etc., you will find relief from stress, discover inner strength, enhance emotional management and focus, and ultimately unleash your imagination and creativity. By practicing multisensory art meditation, you can elevate your quality of life and happiness, rediscover yourself, and pave the way for your spiritual growth.

This book is a portable workshop on multisensory art & meditation, offering the potential for profound transformation. The introductory chapter covers the basics, and the following six chapters delve into specific topics for exploration and practice. You can read from the beginning or start with the chapters that interest you the most. By practicing one chapter per week, you will experience a profound transformation within a month and a half.

At the beginning of each chapter, I will introduce content from the classical Eastern philosophy of the Dao De Jing that has inspired me, combined with my insights and experiences from living in the West. Additionally, each chapter will include my art pieces, which you could meditate on, and related stories and concepts related to the work. Through these engaging multisensory art meditations, you will get some ideas about multisensory art and gradually learn about the connections between colors and emotions, chakras and energy, essential oil aromatherapy, and the basics of the wu xing & feng shui.

At the end of each chapter, I have designed a comprehensive exercise to guide you in applying these diverse elements in your daily life, creating your own multisensory art and meditation practice. Following the suggestions for combining the exercises will unlock your creativity and expressiveness, eventually developing your unique meditation art series.

Whether you are an art enthusiast, a meditation practitioner, or someone seeking to enhance your quality of life, this book will offer you a new perspective and experience. Regardless of your challenges and difficulties, I hope you find a path to inner peace through art and meditation, improve your quality of life, and discover a serene oasis amid your busy life, living a more meaningful and fulfilling life.

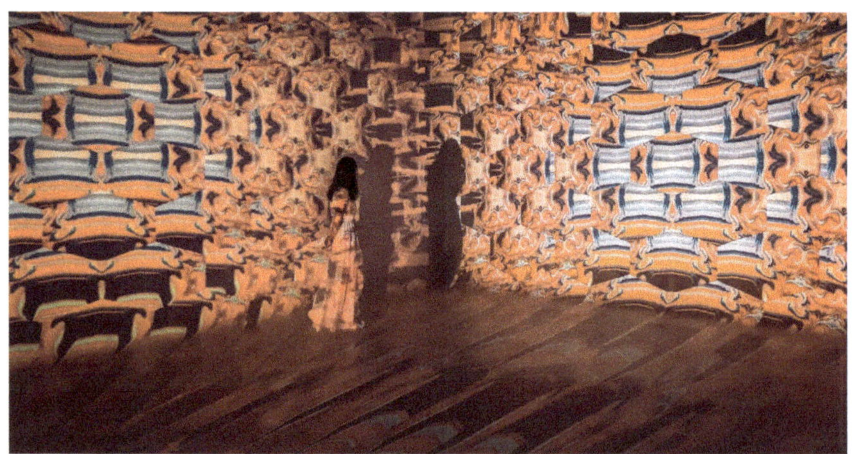

Kaleidoscopic Meditation, Pebblebed, San Francisco, 2023

Multisensory Art + Meditation

Multisensory Art is the term I use to describe my artistic approach.
It integrates Eastern and Western cultures, drawing on traditional Eastern philosophy and meditation techniques while employing interactive technology. This is not merely art to be admired; it is a timeless spatial art installation that invites viewers to engage and interact, offering a sensory feast that merges body and soul. This art form, born from the artistic design knowledge I've gleaned from both East and West, my architectural background, and personal growth experiences, is truly immersive. It incorporates elements of color, sound, scent, touch, and feng shui to transform any space into an immersive art installation, creating a unique environment for the audience.

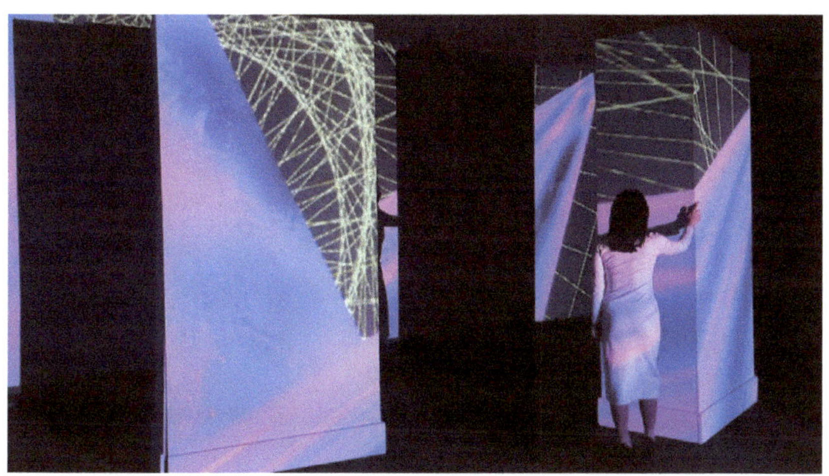

Lost in Purple, Multisensory Art Installation, San Francisco, 2023

Through multisensory stimulation, viewers can resonate more deeply with the artwork, leading to a meditative state. Research shows that multisensory stimulation has positive effects on psychological and physiological health. Combining visual, auditory, olfactory, and tactile senses can relieve stress, improve mood, enhance focus, and boost creativity. Therefore, Multisensory Art not only provides aesthetic enjoyment but also offers significant benefits for mental health. By appreciating this art form, one can achieve relaxation, enrich sensory experiences, and unlock more potential.

My Life Journey and My Art

My journey in creating multisensory art began at the Rhode Island School of Design (RISD). Before enrolling, I always believed that the various specialized fields in design and art were isolated. Despite my wide range of interests, during my studies in urban planning, I never imagined combining my hobbies of guzheng performance, music composition, or perfume collection with my design and art.

Until I went to RISD, the interdisciplinary atmosphere inspired me and made me realize there are no absolute boundaries. Constant exploration and innovation can reshape unique ideas and even redefine life. Therefore, during my studies at RISD, I focused on architecture and actively took courses in cross-disciplines. These diverse learning experiences deepened my understanding of design and art.

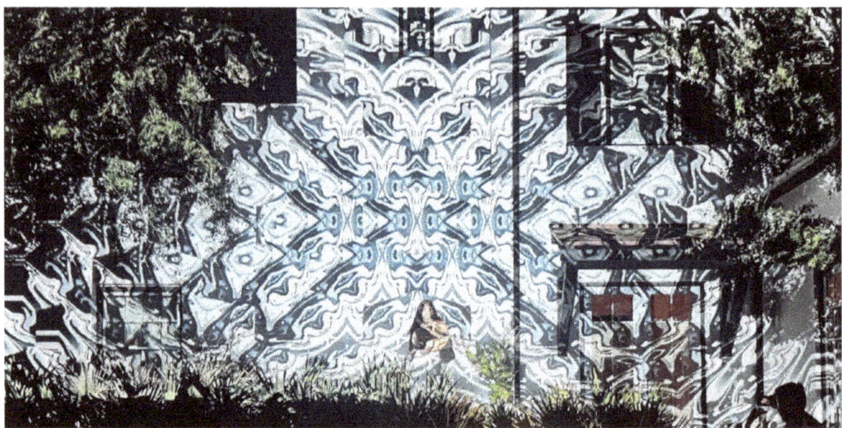

Kaleidoscopic Meditation , Digital Graffiti, Florida, 2023

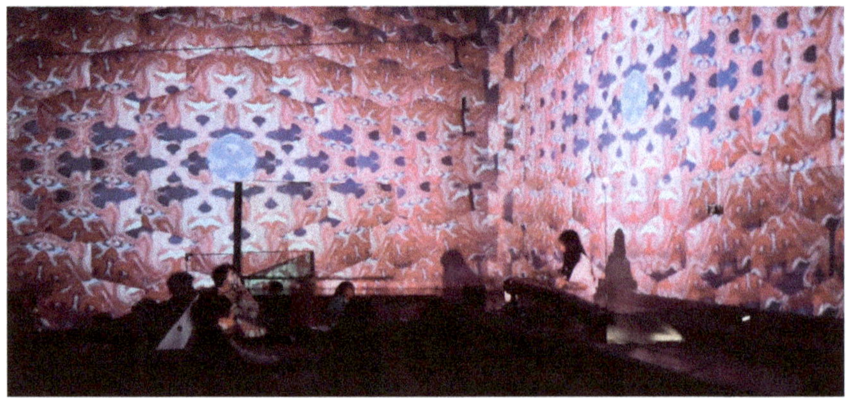

Floating Dream -Live Immersive & Interactive Art Performance and Solo Exhibition, San Francisco, 2023

I am most grateful for the education I received in the architecture department. It opened the door to the world of design and art for me and instilled in me the qualities of perseverance and patience in exploring the underlying logic of things. These experiences laid a solid foundation for my subsequent explorations. Although studying in the architecture department was exceptionally challenging, I developed my unique understanding of materials, structures, aesthetics, forms, design logic, etc., through intensive professional training.

All of this is thanks to my professors, Kyna Leski, Hansy Better, Carl Lostritto, and Christopher Bardt. They have profoundly impacted my design philosophy and thinking. I especially want to mention Professors Kyna Leski and Hansy Better, who, as outstanding female architects and educators, have set a model for my growth as a female artist and designer.

Additionally, Professor Daniel Lefcourt's "Drawing and Innovation" course was an introductory course for me to the art world. Throughout the course, he encouraged us to forget existing knowledge constraints and experiment with different media and forms of expression to unleash our creativity. This course introduced me to many new concepts. It broadened my horizons, making me realize that art should not be confined to specific forms but should exist vibrantly in various unexpected states.

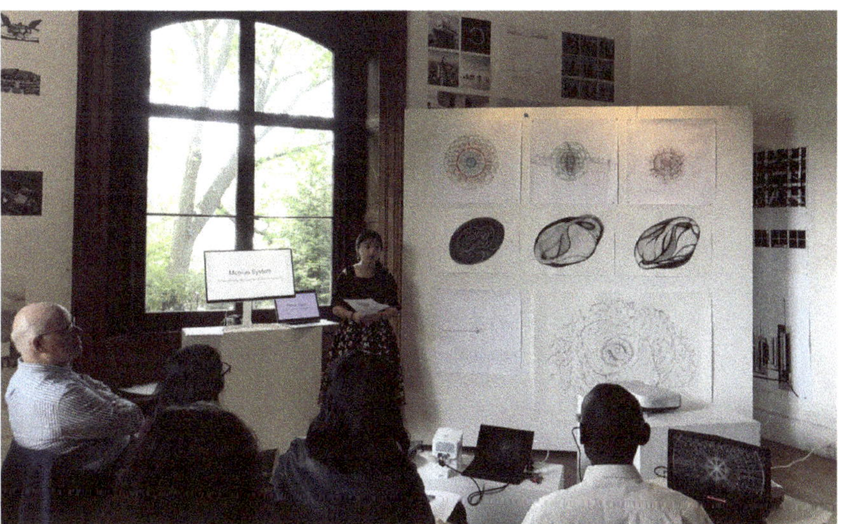

Critique for My Thesis, Möbius system, RISD, 2018

At RISD, I was fortunate to meet classmates from various academic backgrounds. They were not only talented but also exceptionally hardworking. Their bold innovations inspired me to be courageous in my creative explorations. These experiences enriched my academic abilities and enabled me to continue advancing in my life explorations and personal creations.

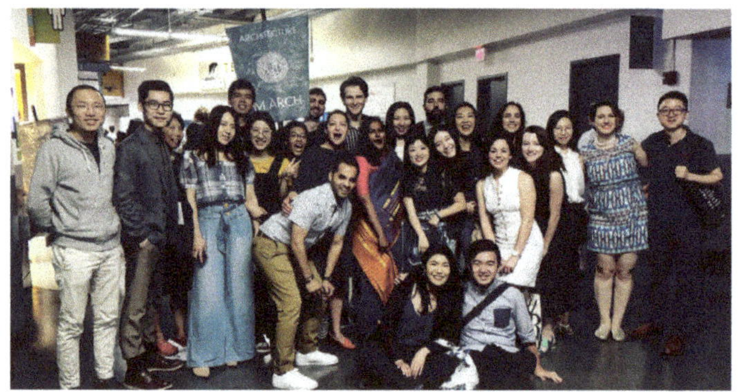

Architecture Department, RISD Commencement 2018

In 2018, I graduated from the architecture program at the RISD. After completing several art exhibitions in Boston and Providence, I moved to New York to work as a full-time architectural designer and a senior researcher in biological structures and parametric design. In the New Lab at Brooklyn Navy Yard, I get other life inspiration, too. The co-founder of Terreform ONE, Dr. Mitchell Joachim, and the Executive Director, Vivian Kuan, greatly inspired me with the innovative thinking and excellent leadership. I learned the concept of design impact and the comprehensive abilities required of an outstanding design leader.

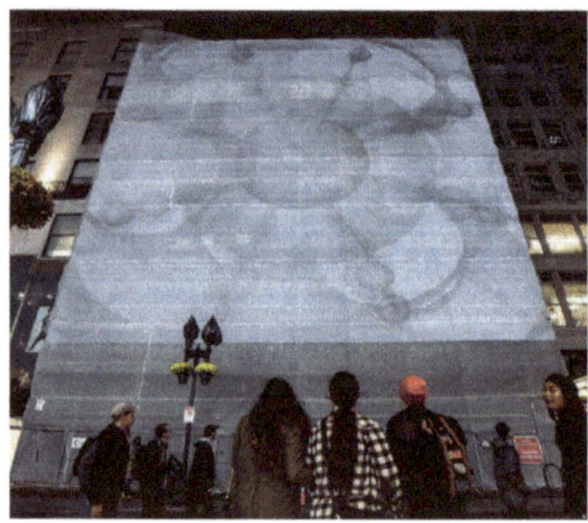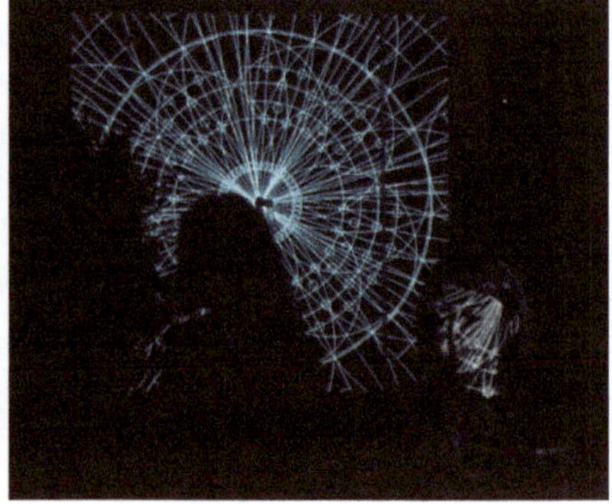

My Art Exhibitions at Boston and Florida, 2018-2019

During my time in the Lab, I had the opportunity to collaborate with scientists, designers, and engineers from Harvard, MIT, Princeton, and other prestigious institutions. We studied monarch butterflies' biological structure and habits and analyzed and restructured this information and data. We integrated these biological structures into ecological architectural design, creating the unprecedented design project Monarch Sanctuary against this specific species' extinction, which was eventually exhibited at the Cooper Hewitt Design Museum. This project later won the 2019 Architizer A+ Award.

It was featured by BBC, Architectural Digest, The Architect's Newspaper, and other renowned media. This unique work experience provided numerous opportunities to contemplate cross-disciplinary collaboration and innovative design research methods, subsequently influencing my design concept and research approach.

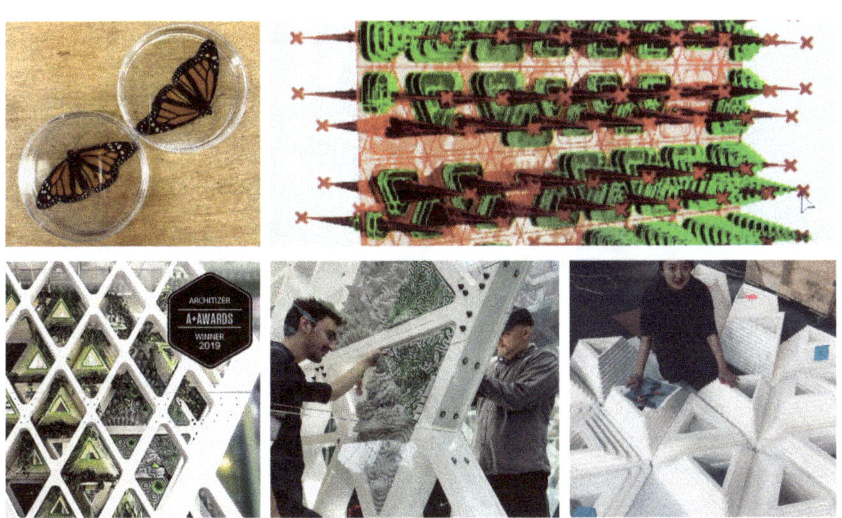

Monarch Sanctuary, Terreform ONE, New York, 2018-2019

After leaving the lab, I decided to explore a new life. My life and focus have always revolved around urban planning and architectural design over the twelve years of my undergraduate, graduate, and professional studies. This singular focus limited my understanding of other dimensions of society and hindered my exploration of alternative life possibilities. I knew that a singular life experience could lead to personal development constraints. To enrich my perspective and expertise, I engaged in various new explorations to fill these gaps: I participated in several hackathons, learning to drive projects as a team leader.

I worked as a curator to plan and host educational summits and art exhibitions to experience the process from concept to reality. Later, I founded a non-profit organization in New York that served as a cultural exchange and knowledge-sharing platform, organizing cultural and academic seminars and events for two years. Based on this non-profit, I also created a business networking website called Synking. Through these endeavors, I honed my leadership and project planning skills. I was fortunate to interact with numerous talented individuals from diverse backgrounds—some of them are renowned writers, scientists, successful entrepreneurs, film directors, etc. Each event was meticulously prepared, and I engaged in deep conversations with these experts, helping me understand the significance of collaboration and exchange. Through them, I saw a broader world.

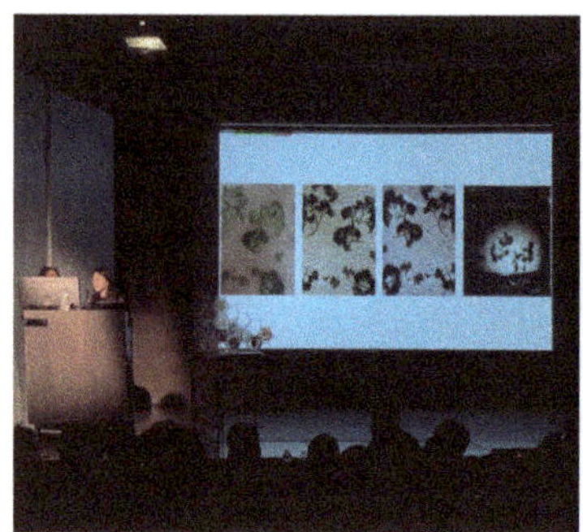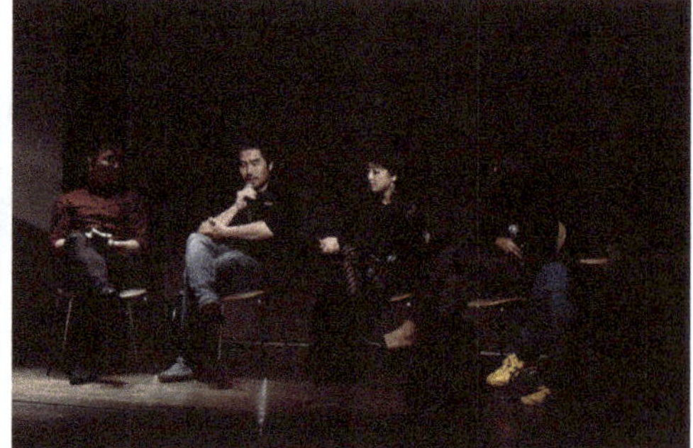

Bio-Material of Senses Presentation at Material Research & Design Symposium, Copper Union, New York, 2019

At the peak of this platform's success, I encountered a new life inspiration through an exceptional collaborator—Dixia Fan, a fluid dynamics scientist from MIT. Our conversations were engaging, leading us to collaborate on a STEAM (Science, Technology, Engineering, Arts, Mathematics) K12 education project. We quickly assembled a team, inviting designers and scientists from Harvard, UPenn, MIT, and RISD to participate in building this project. Drawing on Dixia's course design for MIT first-year students, we developed a bipedal robot design course for Chinese elementary school students. This course was successfully introduced to eight public schools in Shanghai, receiving much acclaim.

We faced numerous challenges throughout this process, but working with Dixia is inspiring. He is a brilliant, talented scientist and an outstanding leader with a great personality. His resilience and wisdom always motivated and attracted people to create together. He showed me the qualities not just of a great scholar but a remarkable entrepreneur and should have.

The onset of the pandemic marked a turning point in my life, bringing with it the most painful insight I had ever experienced. My entrepreneurial projects struggled due to the pandemic, and funding efforts were unsuccessful. Unfortunately, I also contracted COVID-19. Amid anxiety and pain, I had to make the difficult decision to disband my team and halt my work. During my most challenging times, my emotional struggles and psychological stress led to countless intense arguments with my ex, which caused further trauma. After enduring a devastating breakup and the painful failure of my startup, I hit rock bottom. "Everything in my life is ruined," I often thought during those days. In those moments of deep emotional turmoil, no amount of comfort from friends and family seemed to soothe my heart. I felt as though I had locked myself in a bottomless dark room, enveloped in a state of profound sorrow, continuously hurting and tormenting my body and soul.

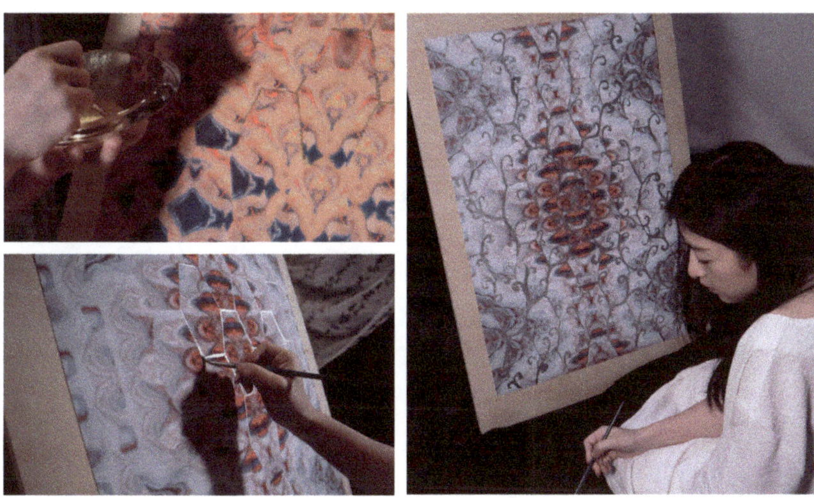

Kaleidoscopic Meditation - Drawings, San Francisco, 2022

In that moment, art emerged as the sole beam of light capable of piercing through the darkness. It soothed and guided me to see the delicate child in my heart. Ultimately, I distilled my style and approach to art and design through the endurance of prolonged suffering and pain.

During this period of isolation, art felt like a reset button in my life. It provided me with an opportunity for deep reflection and self-dialogue. I also practiced meditation and yoga in the creation process, revisiting some ancient Eastern philosophical texts.

These ancient wisdoms helped me reconnect with my cultural roots. Slowly, I found the energy to review and organize my past experiences, combining my music, art, and fragrance skills to develop my expression method. I deeply felt the soothing power of this form of meditative art on my soul.

Throughout this process, it repeatedly helped me heal myself. When emotions arose, they were no longer burdens; instead, they transformed into creative inspiration. Expressing these through art has also become a way to heal others.

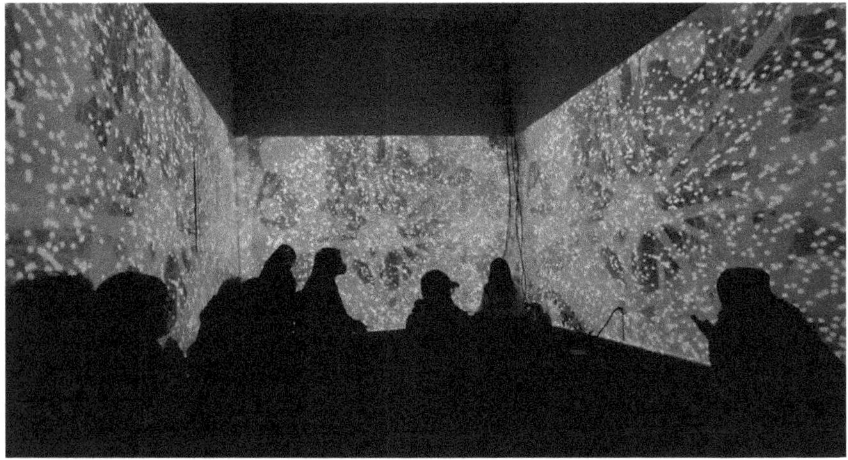
Zhunagzi's Butterfly Inception, Gray Area, San Francisco, 2023

Looking back, I am so grateful for these life experiences and the people who have inspired me from different perspectives. These experiences have deepened my understanding beyond art, design, culture, and technology—they have also deepened my understanding of life.

As an Asian female artist and entrepreneur, I have experienced many challenges in my life. In my growing process, no one taught me how to deal with this trauma and how to recover. However, my life and mindset have changed dramatically through the consistent creation and practice of multisensory art and meditation.

Over the years, I have successfully exhibited multisensory art exhibitions globally, extending my concept into a designer brand that serves more people through products. In my art exhibitions and live performances worldwide, I have met many audiences who have experienced personal growth, inner peace, and pleasure. They were inspired to start this journey from watching art to creating art, reflecting on it, and rediscovering themselves.

The favorable reviews and feedback I have received from my personal experiences and exhibitions inspired me to introduce multisensory art and meditation to a broader audience.

In an age of prevalent AI-generated material, it is very easy to get lost. therefore, it is essential to treasure your unique identity. Understanding who you are and what you want to become is a profound and personal journey that no AI can undertake for you.

By experiencing and creating multisensory art and meditation, you can reflect on yourself and evoke your potential. I hope you find inner peace and rediscover yourself through "Artful Awakening."

Xinye Lin
2024 .7

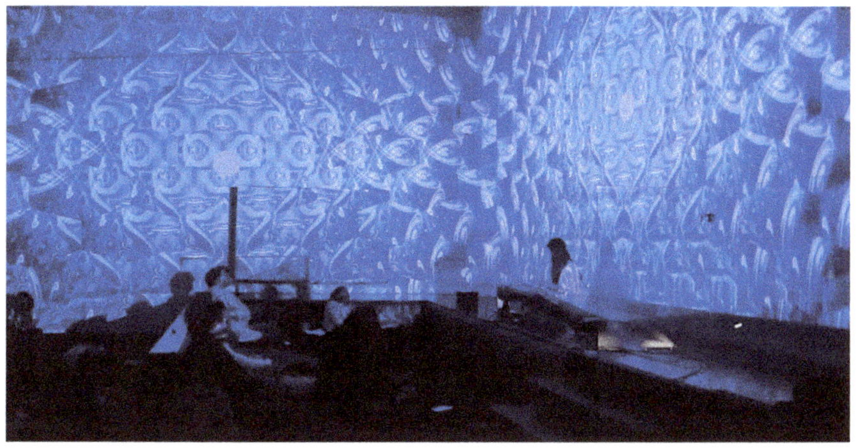

Floating Dream -Live Immersive & Interactive Art Performance and Solo Exhibition, San Francisco, 2023

ARTWORKS SELECTED FOR THE BOOK

KALEIDOSCOPIC MEDITATION SERIES

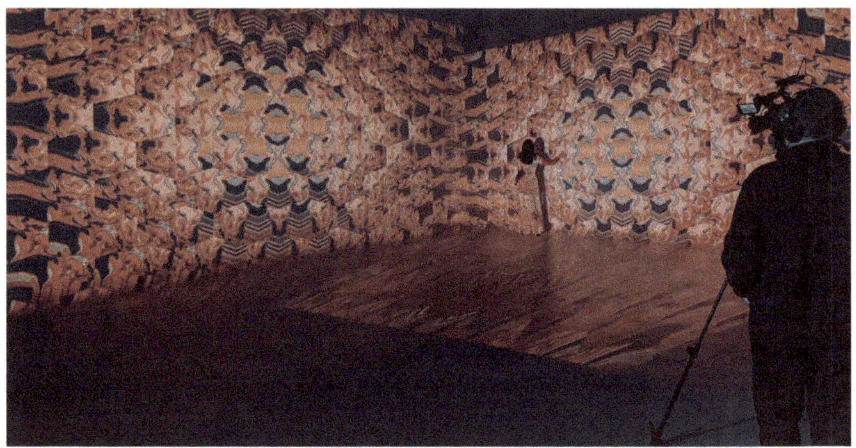

Kaleidoscopic Meditation is a series of multi-sensory immersive artworks for meditation by Artist Xinye Lin. Deeply inspired by classical Asian culture, Xinye's creative inspiration comes from the essence of Asian classical studies, profound experiences in personal meditation, and her background in architecture and other fields such as music and art.

Xinye uses art to document her abstract feelings while reading Eastern philosophy and cultural stories and meditating. She transforms these abstract emotions into tangible artworks. She incorporates interactive technology and geometric algorithms to inject a dynamic soul into static creations, facilitating real-time interactions and resonance between the artwork and emotions, sounds, smells, and spaces.

This series has been presented in various forms, including dynamic, immersive interactive art & live music performances, and static visual art exhibitions.

In the immersive and interactive version of exhibitions, the artist transforms the ordinary space into an entire art installation by using her expertise in architectural design & scent design, 3D projection mapping, interactive technology, as well as impromptu performances on instruments like the guzheng, Tibetan singing bowls, and MIDI as mediums, triggering dialogues between the art and music, leading the viewers through auditory, visual, olfactory, tactile, and spatial perceptions into a meditative, dream-like state, allowing them to immerse themselves in a beautiful, healing atmosphere and experience the energy flow of meditation.

Moreover, selected frames of animations from live performances are carefully chosen for high-precision printing as part of the static exhibition. Each image captures a moment in time, representing memories sealed in time within "Kaleidoscopic Meditation."

These artworks aim to create unforgettable, fantasy-colored, multi-sensory art experiences, allowing viewers to experience a healing atmosphere in this unspoken beauty, forget worldly worries, and find inner peace and harmony.

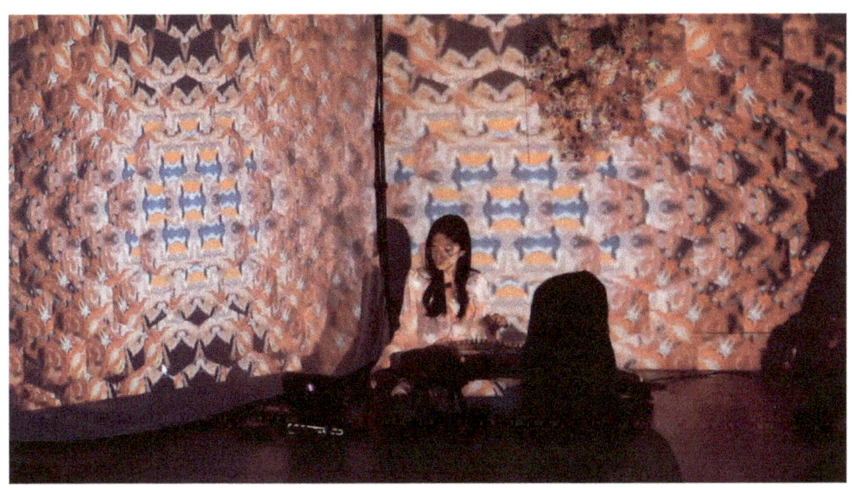

CHAPTER I
MULTISENSORY ART MEDITATION

BASIC CONCEPTS AND APPLICATIONS

In the age of information overload, we are constantly bombarded with notifications, news, and updates that often lack significance, leaving us feeling overwhelmed and anxious. This relentless barrage makes it difficult to calm our minds, listen to our inner voices, and discover our inner strength. Excessive stress and anxiety can hinder our abilities, making it challenging to accomplish our goals. This book will harness the power of art and meditation to awaken your senses, help you rediscover yourself, and foster a deep connection within, leading to profound transformation.

Research shows that multisensory art meditation can significantly reduce stress and anxiety, enhance emotional regulation, and boost creativity and focus. A 2018 study by Harvard University found that meditation practices incorporating multisensory stimuli significantly improve psychological resilience and overall well-being (Harvard Health Publishing, 2018). These findings underscore the potential of multisensory art meditation to transform our daily lives. Integrating multiple sensory stimuli, this method comprehensively activates our senses, enhancing mental and physical health.

This book is an artist's personal growth journal and a practical workshop on multisensory art and meditation. Through multisensory art, you will experience meditation and knowledge across various disciplines and explore your preferred forms of meditative art creation. Throughout this journey, you will get ideas about stimulating your senses. This process will help you relieve stress and inspire you to experience life differently.

Ultimately, It will unleash your imagination and creativity, improve your quality of life and well-being, and help you rediscover yourself in a new light.

Before our journey, please let me introduce some basic concepts related to this book. If you are already familiar with these concepts, feel free to skip this chapter.

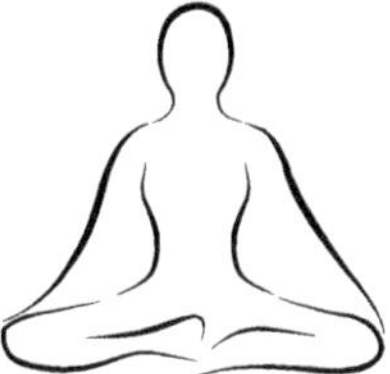

What is Meditation

Meditation is an ancient, powerful, non-religious practice that guides us into deep consciousness through quiet and focused contemplation. It has various forms and dates back thousands of years, but the core goal remains to achieve inner peace and balance by controlling attention and breath.

Meditation is not just a relaxation technique but a journey of self-discovery. It teaches us to establish a genuine connection with ourselves, delving deep into our minds to uncover hidden emotions and thoughts. Through meditation, we learn to observe our thoughts and emotions without being influenced, cultivating a sense of tranquility and insight.

Modern society teaches us numerous skills for surviving and thriving in the external world. Still, few genuinely teach us how to explore our inner world, connect with ourselves, how to understand and accept ourselves. Meditation is such a tool, providing a pathway to delve deep within and recognize ourselves.

Benefits of Meditation

Stress Relief Through artistic creation and meditation, we can release inner anxiety and stress, achieving a state of physical and mental relaxation. According to a study in Psychological Science, regular meditation can significantly lower cortisol levels, reducing stress (Tang, Hölzel, & Posner, 2015).

Creativity Boost When we meditate, our minds become more open and flexible, sparking more creative thinking. A study by Stanford University found that meditation can enhance brain connectivity, promoting creative problem-solving (Colzato, Ozturk, & Hommel, 2012).

Enhanced Focus Artistic meditation requires us to fully concentrate on the current creative process, training our focus, which helps us perform tasks more effectively in daily life.

Long-term Mental Health Benefits Art allows us to express our inner emotions and thoughts, which can profoundly impact our mental well-being.

Increased Happiness The sense of achievement from art creation and the inner peace from meditation can enhance our overall happiness.

Nurturing the Inner Child Through meditation, we can reach the pure and childlike part of our inner self, nourishing and bringing joy to our inner child, thus better cooperating with ourselves.

Improved Sleep Quality Regular meditation can be a powerful tool for relaxing the mind and body, reducing anxiety, and promoting better sleep.

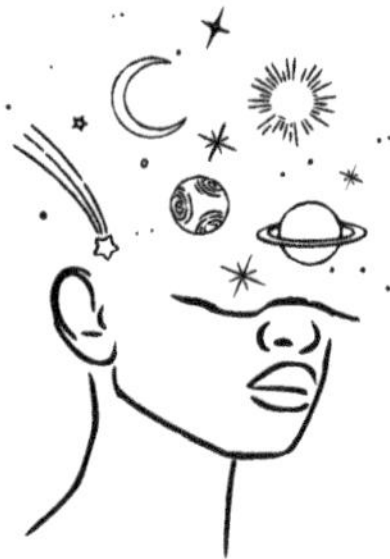

Core Elements iof Meditation

- Focused Breathing: By focusing on the rhythm of breathing, we can concentrate our attention and reduce distractions.

- Mindfulness: During meditation, maintain awareness of the present moment without judging your thoughts and emotions, simply observing.

- Physical Relaxation: Find a comfortable posture to fully relax your body, aiding in entering a deep meditative state.

- Inner Calm: Through meditation, cultivate inner peace and tranquility unaffected by external disturbances.

Relaxation Techniques and Postures Before Meditation

Engaging in some simple relaxation techniques and postures before meditation can help you enter a meditative state more effectively.

Relaxation Techniques:

- Deep Breathing: Before meditation, engage in a few minutes of deep breathing to help relax the mind and body. Deeply inhale through your nose, feeling your abdomen rise, then slowly exhale through your mouth, feeling your abdomen fall.

- Progressive Muscle Relaxation: Start from your toes and work up to your head, focusing on one area at a time, tensing for a few seconds, then relaxing. This technique helps you recognize tension spots and gradually relaxes the whole body.

- Breath Observation: Before meditating, focus on your breath, observing each inhale and exhale rhythm and depth without controlling it—observe. This technique helps focus attention and enter a meditative state.

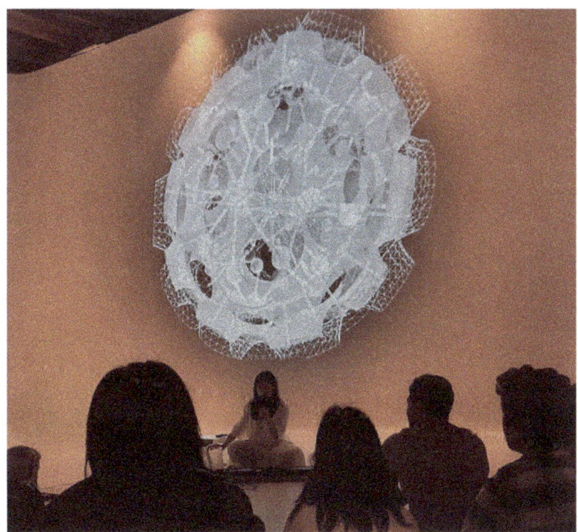
breathing while chanting
Live Performance at Pebblebed,San Francisco, 2023

Relaxation Postures:

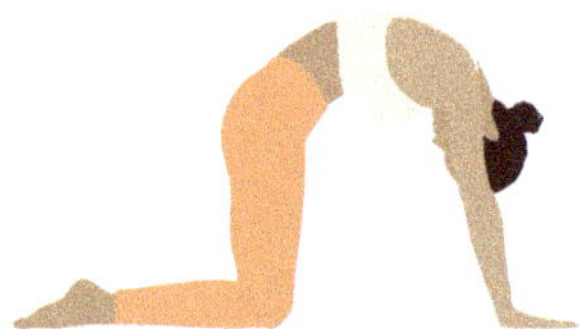

Cat-Cow Pose
This yoga pose helps relax the spine and back muscles by bending and extending the back. Place your hands and knees on the ground. Inhale as you bend your back, look up, and exhale as you arch your back towards your navel.

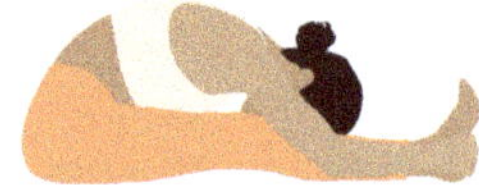

Seated Forward Bend
Sit on the ground with legs straight. Inhale, raise your arms, exhale, and bend forward, reaching for your toes. This pose stretches the back and leg muscles, helping to relax the body.

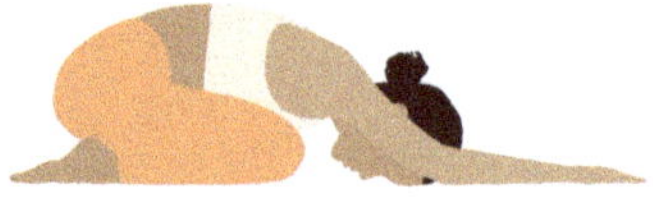

Child's Pose
Kneel on the ground, with feet together and knees apart. Exhale, bend forward, place your forehead on the ground, and let your arms relax beside your body. This pose calms the back and shoulders, relieving stress.

Common Breathing Techniques During Meditation

Proper breathing techniques during meditation can help you enter a meditative state more quickly and enhance the effects of meditation.

- Abdominal Breathing: This breathing method helps deep relaxation. Feel your abdomen rise as you inhale and fall as you exhale. Deep breathing like this can better relax the body and mind, reducing tension.

- Alternate Nostril Breathing: This technique balances the activity of the left and right brain. Use your right thumb to close your right nostril, inhale through your left nostril, then use your right ring finger to close your left nostril and exhale through your right nostril. Then, switch directions, repeating a few times.

- 4-7-8 Breathing: This technique helps reduce anxiety and stress. Inhale for 4 seconds, hold for 7 seconds and then exhale slowly for 8 seconds. Repeat a few times, feeling your body gradually relax.

Concepts for Multisensory Art & Meditation

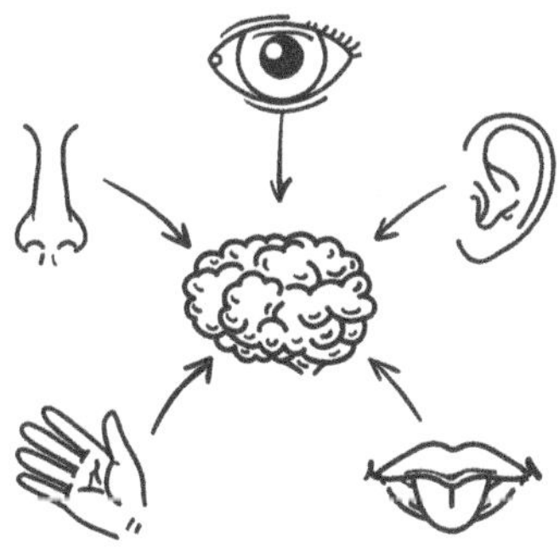

Color and Senses: The Power of Vision

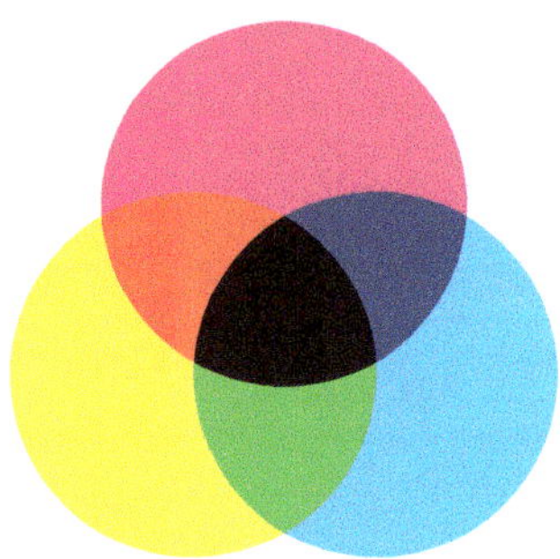

The role of color in meditation should not be underestimated. Different colors can lead us into various emotional states, aiding relaxation and focus through visual stimuli. Colors profoundly impact our psychological and emotional well-being, each carrying unique vibrations and frequencies that influence our mood and mental state.

Cool tones such as blue, green, purple, and white are associated with tranquility, relaxation, and inner balance. These colors help reduce stress, promote mental calmness, and enhance spiritual awareness. Warm tones like yellow, red, and orange relate to energy, passion, and positive emotions, boosting mood, creativity, and motivation.

Neutral tones such as gray and brown, bright tones like pink and gold, and dark tones like black also play significant roles in meditation. Gray and brown provide a sense of balance and stability, pink and gold elevate emotional warmth and positive energy, while black promotes deep introspection and the release of the subconscious.

By flexibly using and combining these colors, we can adjust our psychological and emotional states according to specific needs, achieving deeper inner harmony and personal growth. Subsequent chapters will provide specific examples and applications of these colors in meditation.

Chakras and Crystals: Balancing Through Touch

Chakras refer to energy centers within the body, originating from ancient Indian philosophy. The chakra system typically consists of seven main chakras, each associated with specific physiological functions and emotional states. Through meditation and other practices, we can activate and balance these chakras, promoting physical and mental health. Crystal healing is a therapy that uses the energy of crystals to enhance physical and mental well-being. Different types of crystals have different energy frequencies that can influence our emotions, mental state, and physical health. Using crystals in meditation can enhance the effects of meditation and help balance chakra energy.

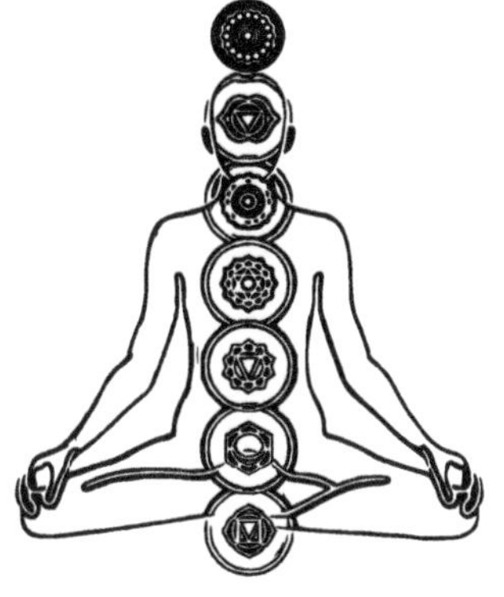

- Root Chakra (Muladhara): Located at the base of the spine, representing survival and basic security. Its color is red, which is associated with the earth element.
- Sacral Chakra (Svadhisthana): Located below the navel, representing creativity and emotion. Its color is orange, associated with the water element.
- Solar Plexus Chakra (Manipura): Located in the stomach area, representing personal power and self-esteem. Its color is yellow, associated with the fire element.
- Heart Chakra (Anahata): Located at the center of the chest, representing love and compassion. Its color is green, associated with the air element.
- Throat Chakra (Vishuddha): Located at the throat, representing expression and communication. Its color is blue, associated with the ether element.
- Third Eye Chakra (Ajna): Located at the forehead, representing intuition and wisdom. Its color is indigo, associated with the light element.
- Crown Chakra (Sahasrara): Located at the top of the head, representing spiritual connection and enlightenment. Its color is violet or white, associated with cosmic energy.

Essential Oils and Fragrances: The Healing Power of Smell

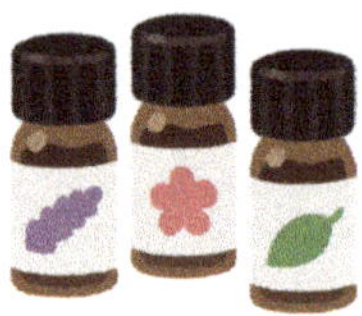

Aromatherapy plays an essential role in meditation. Different essential oils influence emotions and psychological states through the olfactory system, helping us relax and enhance the meditation experience.

Aromatherapy uses plant essential oils to promote physical and mental health. These oils enter the brain through the olfactory system, influencing emotions, memory, and hormone balance, achieving therapeutic and relaxing effects. Aromatherapy's application in meditation can enhance the meditation experience, helping relax the body and mind and elevating mood.

Feng Shui and Wuxing: Creating a Harmonious Meditation Space

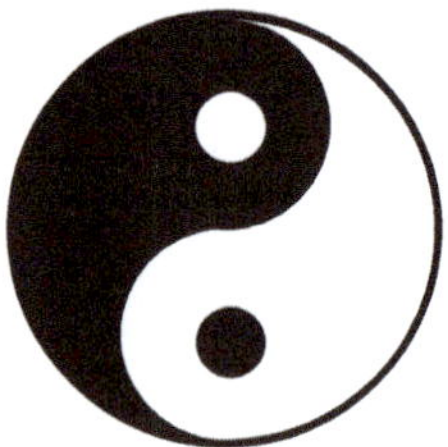

Feng Shui is an ancient Chinese practice that studies the influence of the environment on people. It aims to improve personal and family fortune and health through environmental arrangements. Feng Shui focuses on the energy flow in nature, achieving harmony and balance through appropriate layouts and decorations, enhancing life quality. The effects of meditation can be enhanced through the rational arrangement of the meditation space. Choosing a quiet space and using appropriate colors and decorations can create an ideal environment for meditation, life, and work.

Wuxing - Five Elements Theory
Feng Shui's five elements theory includes wood, fire, earth, metal, and water. These elements interact to maintain balance in the universe and humans. By using the five elements wisely, energy flow in the environment can be adjusted and improved.

- Wood: Represents growth and vitality, usually associated with green and the east.

- Fire: Represents passion and energy, usually associated with red and the south.

- Earth: Represents stability and foundation, usually associated with yellow and the center.

- Metal: Represents purity and harvest, usually associated with white and the west.

- Water: Represents wisdom and flow, usually associated with blue and the north.

How to Use This Book

While reading this book, I hope you can establish your meditation habit by choosing a fixed meditation time, starting with 5-15 minutes.

There are six chapters that focus on different topics, and each chapter has one week of practice time. To start practicing, you can choose the part you are most concerned about or want to strengthen or follow the order in the book.

If time is limited, you can skip the creating practice and only follow the multisensory art meditation practice in each chapter.

Steps for practice:

- Set a Fixed Meditation Time: Choose a fixed weekly time for the practice.

- Prepare for Meditation: Find a quiet, comfortable place, ensuring this place is free from disturbances. Scan the QR code and practice along with the video for each chapter. A projector or a large TV screen is suggested to create an immersive experience.

- Start Meditating: Start with 5 minutes, gradually increasing to 15 minutes. Treat it as a relaxation and a particular date for yourself. During this time, you can explore different ideas suggested in each chapter.

- Increase Frequency and Persevere: Meditate to gradually develop a stable habit even if the time is short. Also, increase the frequency from weekly to daily. Considering that you may find it challenging to focus for long periods at the beginning or encounter busy times, I have designed a series of 1-3 minute mini-meditation podcasts to help you warm up and maintain daily meditation habits. You can scan the code for my Mini Meditation podcast.

- Join the Community: Join the Artful Awakening group to connect with creative spirits, share your experiences, and grow together. Scan the QR code to find the discussion group for Artful Awakening and meet creative spirits worldwide.

Scan to access additional resources for this book

linxinye.com/artful-awakening

CHAPTER I

Through the introduction of basic concepts and techniques, I hope you have a preliminary understanding of meditation and multisensory art. I will detail various concepts and knowledge through my artworks and the designed meditation practices in the following chapters.

You can experience the charm of multisensory meditation art through regular practice, giving yourself a mental massage.

Let's start this six weeks' magic journey together now :)

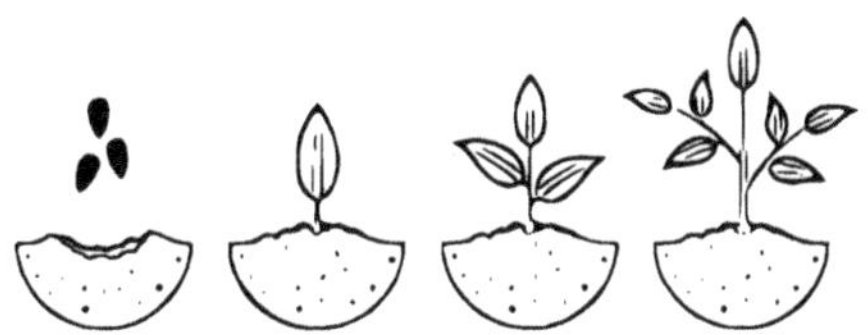

References
- Harvard Health Publishing. (2018). The benefits of mindfulness meditation.
- Tang, Y. Y., Hölzel, B. K., & Posner, M. I. (2015). The neuroscience of mindfulness meditation. Nature Reviews Neuroscience, 16(4), 213-225.
- Colzato, L. S., Ozturk, A., & Hommel, B. (2012). Meditate to create: the impact of focused-attention and openmonitoring training on convergent and divergent thinking. Frontiers in Psychology, 3, 116.

CHAPTER II
RELAXATION AND STRESS RELIEF

ENHANCING THE SENSES AND UNLEASHING POTENTIAL

Have you noticed how your body and senses react under the most pressure and stress? How does it affect your emotional state?

> ## Do nothing, and nothing will be left undone
> —Dao De Jing, Chapter 37

This ancient wisdom from Chapter 37 of the Dao De Jing teaches us to achieve everything in a relaxed mind. Wu Wei (non-action) means doing nothing; instead, it means approaching life with a natural and peaceful attitude, not being troubled by external pressures and distractions, thereby achieving the best self without deliberate effort.

This state is crucial for modern life as we are often constrained by stress and tension, losing inner peace and sensory acuity. Relaxing the mind can help us better cope with the complexities and pressures of modern life.

Interpretation and Extension

"Wu Wei" emphasizes going with the flow and following the natural course of events rather than forcibly controlling and changing. In modern life, we often become anxious and tense due to pressure and stress. This state not only affects our mental health but also dulls our sensory acuity and inner strength. By relaxing the mind, we can reduce inner anxiety and stress, restoring inner peace and harmony.

During the process of relaxing the mind, "Wu Wei" is a key attitude. Wu Wei is not passive inaction but actively letting go of attachments to external things and facing life's challenges with a peaceful heart. Our inner strength naturally emerges when we relax and are no longer driven by external pressures.

For example, in artistic creation, when we no longer strive for perfection but focus on the process and feelings, we often inspire more profound creativity and inspiration.

Relaxing the mind also helps us better perceive and experience the world. By reducing inner distractions and clutter, we can more keenly sense our surroundings. This keen perception ability not only aids our artistic creation but also enhances our quality of life and happiness.

The Harm of Stress

Stress and tension are almost ubiquitous in life. Whether in studies, work, or various aspects of life, we feel physically and mentally exhausted. The fast pace and high demands of modern society have significantly increased our pressure.

Studies show that people today generally endure more significant psychological stress than ever before. For instance, according to a survey report by the American Psychological Association (APA), nearly 70% of adults report experiencing significant stress. This high-stress environment affects our emotions and mental health and negatively impacts our physical health, including insomnia, digestive issues, and weakened immunity.

While moderate stress can stimulate our potential and lead to exceptional performance in some situations, prolonged high-stress states seriously threaten our physical health. A study by Stanford University found that sustained high-stress environments weaken the hippocampus, which is responsible for learning and memory and affects our cognitive and innovative abilities.

Additionally, stress leads to poor sleep quality, further impacting our sensory acuity and overall health. Long-term stress can cause rigid thinking, frequent mood swings, and even emotional breakdowns. Sustained high stress diminishes our imagination and creativity and makes it difficult to find new inspiration and solutions, hindering our potential.

The Impact of Multisensory Art Meditation on Stress Relief

Numerous scientific studies have proven that meditation is an effective method for relaxation and stress relief, significantly improving the negative effects of stress. For example, a Harvard University study found that multisensory stimulation in meditation significantly enhances participants' psychological resilience and well-being (Harvard Health Publishing, 2018). Innovative multisensory art meditation not only improves emotional regulation but also enhances brain regions related to emotions and senses, helping us regain sensory acuity and cognitive flexibility. In this process, we can transfer inner anxiety and stress, break rigid thinking patterns, and explore new inspirations and solutions. Multisensory art meditation also allows us to more deeply perceive the world around us, improving our overall quality of life and happiness.

My Experience: Stress Relief and Sensory Reboot

In my journey of creation and entrepreneurship, I have experienced many periods of intense pressure. My work progressed slowly during high-pressure times, inspiration dried up, and I couldn't create satisfactory works or confidently face challenges. I felt extremely frustrated. Nightly insomnia and stomach pain nearly broke me. Realizing the great harm this state caused to my body and mind, I started seeking ways to relax and relieve stress, trying to restore my condition. Combining artistic forms and meditation concepts, I conducted daily self-relaxation exercises and spent time in nature. I designed small exercises to activate my senses during that time. Through daily practice, I carefully recorded and observed changes in my life. Gradually, my sleep quality improved, stomach pain disappeared, and inspiration returned. In this way, I regained inner confidence and creative passion.

By relaxing the mind and reconnecting with nature, I successfully reduced inner anxiety and stress, restored sensory acuity, and rekindled creative passion. This transformation helped me find inner peace and harmony and made me more composed and confident in facing life's challenges.

Multisensory Art Meditation Practice

Please scan the QR to access the artwork for meditation practice.

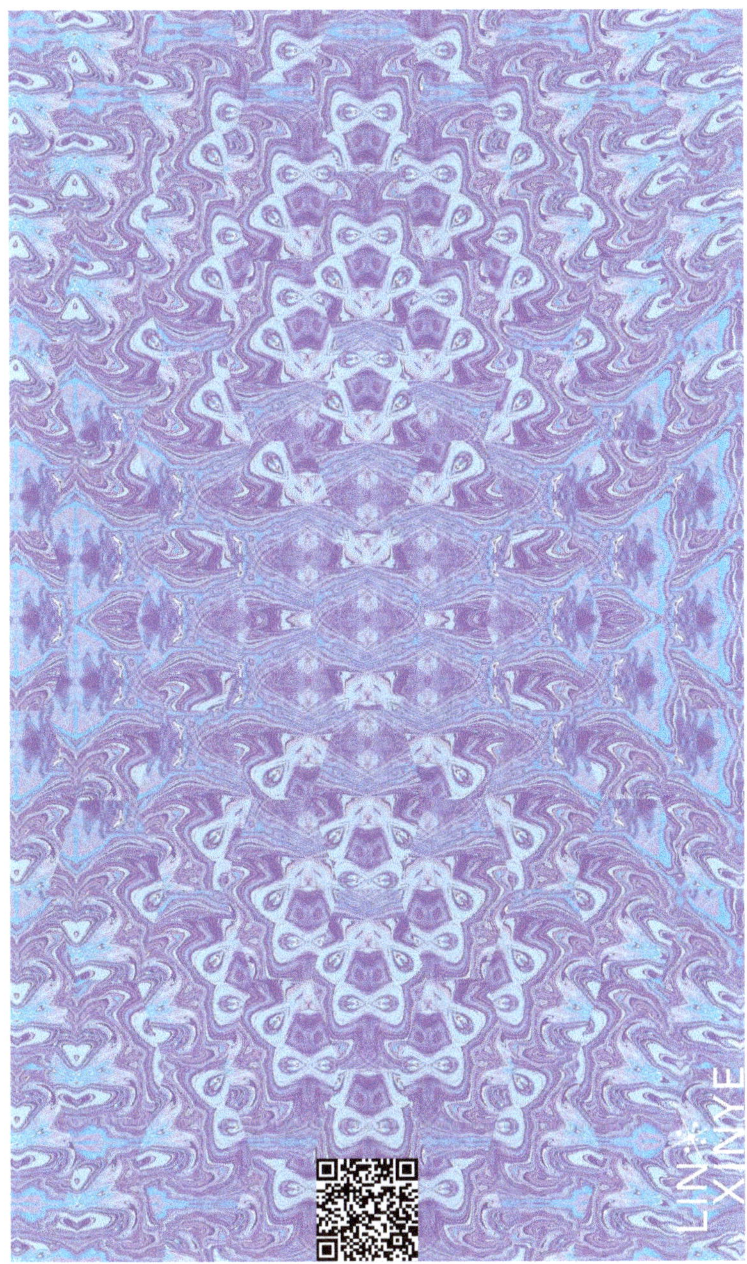

Viewing the artwork in the suggested feng shui direction for a better experience. A projector is recommended to display the artwork on a wall to create a more immersive meditation atmosphere.

Feng Shui Application: Enhancing Energy and Creating a Relaxing Space

Practice in the northern or eastern part of your relaxation space can enhance the peaceful and harmonious energy of the space. Choose a quiet corner of your home as a relaxation space, preferably in the north or east, as these directions are associated with peaceful and tranquil energy. Keep the space clean and tidy to reduce stress and anxiety. Introducing natural elements like plants, stones, and wood can enhance the natural power of the space, helping you relax better. Use soft natural light or warm-toned lighting to create a cozy atmosphere.

In the Wuxing - Five Elements theory, the north is water, and the east is wood. These two directions' energies help nurture our emotions and expressions, respectively. By combining the Five Elements theory, we can better utilize the energies of natural elements and directions to enhance our overall well-being and inner peace.

For this week's multisensory art meditation, you could randomly select one or more of the following to practice together for unexpected benefits.

- Meditation Practice: Close your eyes, breathe deeply, and imagine yourself surrounded by the light of light purple and ocean blue. With each breath, feel the peaceful and harmonious energy entering your body, helping you manage and release stress.
- Aromatherapy: During meditation, light lavender or vanilla essential oil. Let the aroma fill the space, further relaxing your body and mind and enhancing the meditation effect.
- Crystal Use: Touch amethyst and lapis lazuli and feel their energy flow, enhancing the depth of meditation and emotional balance.
- Taste Integration: During meditation, taste a small piece of dark chocolate or a slice of fruit, feeling the changes and layers of taste, further relaxing the body and mind.

Colors Involved in the Artwork

- Purple: Represents tranquility, calmness, and relaxation, helping to relieve stress and enhance inner peace.

- Blue: Symbolizes healing, balance, and rebirth, helping to restore sensory acuity and overall harmony.

Chakras Involved in the Artwork

- Heart Chakra (Anahata): Located at the center of the chest, associated with love and emotions. Meditation on the heart chakra can enhance our emotional expression and acceptance.

- Throat Chakra (Vishuddha): Located at the throat, associated with expression and communication. Meditation on the throat chakra can help us better express and release emotions.

Recommended Essential Oils and Scents for the Artwork

- Lavender: Calming and soothing effects, helping to relieve anxiety and enhance emotional balance.

- Vanilla: A warm and soothing effect, helping to relax the body and mind and enhance happiness.

Related Crystals

- Amethyst: Enhances the energy of the heart chakra, promoting emotional expression and acceptance. Its energy corresponds to the fire element in the Five Elements, enhancing our emotional passion and inner strength.

- Lapis Lazuli: Enhances the energy of the throat chakra, improving expression and emotional release. Its energy corresponds to the wood element in the Five Elements, promoting communication skills and creativity.

Additionally, this week, you can try sensory stimulation exercises through vision, hearing, smell, touch, and taste, randomly selecting one sensory exercise each day to incorporate before and after the formal meditation practice to enhance the effect. Consistent practice can help us deeply experience and understand the world, improve our sensory acuity, and unleash our inner potential.

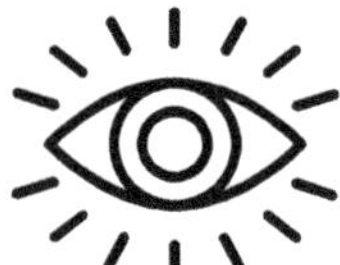

Vision:

- Natural Scenery: Spend time observing natural scenery such as trees, flowers, and the sky to relax the eyes and restore visual acuity.

- Art Appreciation: Regularly visit exhibitions or appreciate artworks to stimulate visual inspiration through colors and composition.

- Color Meditation: Choose soft colors like light purple and ocean blue for meditation to relax the eyes and reduce visual fatigue.

Hearing:

- Natural Sounds: Listen to natural sounds like waves, birdsong, and wind to relax the mind and restore auditory sensitivity.

- Music Meditation: Choose soothing music for meditation, focusing on each note to enhance the auditory experience.

- Sound Therapy: Use different sound frequencies, such as white noise or natural sound effects, to relax and enhance auditory sensitivity.

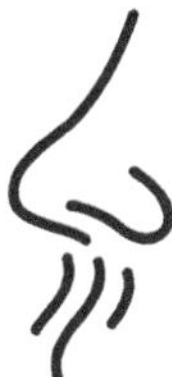

Smell:

- Aromatherapy: Use essential oils like lavender and vanilla to relieve stress and enhance olfactory sensitivity through scent.

- Natural Scents: Frequently engage with natural scents like flowers and trees to relax and restore the sense of smell.

- Deep Breathing: In a fresh air environment, take deep breaths to feel the natural aromas and enhance the olfactory experience.

Touch:

- Touch Natural Materials: Frequently touch natural materials like bark, stones, and sand to feel different textures and enhance the tactile experience.

- Tactile Meditation: During meditation, use objects of different textures for tactile exercises to increase tactile sensitivity.

- Massage Therapy: Use self-massage or professional massage to relax muscles and enhance the tactile experience.

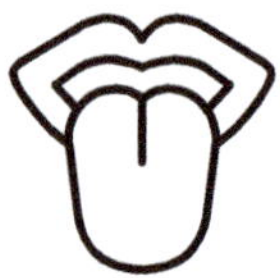

Taste:

- Taste Natural Foods: Slowly savor fresh fruits and vegetables to feel their original taste and enhance taste sensitivity.

- Herbs and Spices: Use different herbs and spices in cooking to experience their unique flavors and stimulate the sense of taste.

- Taste Meditation: During meditation, taste a small piece of chocolate or a slice of fruit, focusing on the sensory experience of taste, feeling its changes and layers.

Creating Time: Art Creation for Unleashing Potential

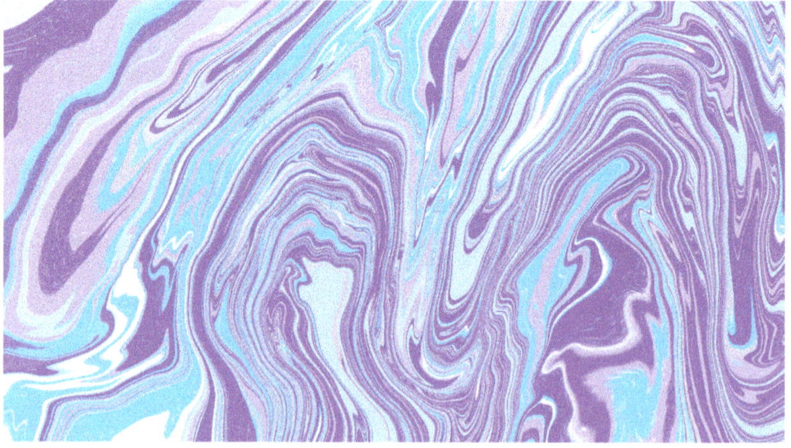

Let's practice a comprehensive exercise to review and master multisensory art meditation. This meditation exercise helps you unleash your inner creativity and create your own artwork.

Steps:

- Prepare Materials: A blank sheet of paper, pencils, or markers - any tools you prefer to draw with, suggest using only two colors.

- Enter Meditation State: Sit in the chosen space, gently close your eyes, take a few deep breaths, and relax all your muscles. Imagine yourself in a place that makes you feel peaceful and sense its atmosphere and energy.

- Start Creating: Open your eyes and freely draw the emotions and inspiration you feel on paper. This can be abstract patterns or specific scenes. Focus on your feelings and emotional expression during the creation process, and don't worry about the outcome; enjoy the process.

- Aromatherapy: During the creation process, light lavender or vanilla essential oil lets the aroma fill the space, further relaxing your body and mind and enhancing the meditation effect.

- End and Record Experience: After finishing the drawing, quietly appreciate your work and record your feelings and experiences. Note the energy changes in the surrounding environment and feel the boost of relaxation and creativity.

In your meditation and artistic creation process, fully utilize these natural elements and energies to help you find inspiration, inner peace, and harmony. Please use them creatively.

Questions and Reflections

- How do you cope with stress and tension in daily life? What new methods can you try to enhance relaxation and stress relief?

- How can relaxation and stress relief help your sensory acuity and creativity?

- How do you use meditation and artistic creation to maintain inner peace and harmony when facing external pressure and inner tension?

By answering these questions and reflecting, you can gain a deeper understanding of your inner world and continue to grow. Document your reflections in a personal notebook. Take time to review them.

You could share your thoughts and art creations with the group.
Connect, get inspired, and grow with other creative spirits.

linxinye.com/group/artful-awakening/
Scan the QR code

References

- Harvard Health Publishing. (2018). The benefits of mindfulness meditation.
- Tang, Y. Y., Hölzel, B. K., & Posner, M. I. (2015). The neuroscience of mindfulness meditation. Nature Reviews Neuroscience, 16(4), 213-225.
- Colzato, L. S., Ozturk, A., & Hommel, B. (2012). Meditate to create: The impact of focused-attention and open-monitoring training on convergent and divergent thinking. Frontiers in Psychology, 3, 116.
- Harvard Health Publishing. (2019). The benefits of multisensory art therapy.

CHAPTER III
INNER STRENGTH

FINDING PEACE AND BALANCE

Can you discern and listen to your inner voice amid the hustle and bustle of life? Have you felt your internal energy field?

> He who knows contentment is rich; he who acts with determination has a strong will.
>
> —Dao De Jing, Chapter 33

This ancient wisdom from the Dao De Jing teaches us the importance of contentment and persistence. The Dao De Jing tells us that those who know contentment are rich in spirit, and those who act with determination have a strong will. In other words, only when we can control and manage our inner selves, finding peace and harmony, can we truly achieve inner strength and stability. This inner strength and peace are key to emotional management and enhancing happiness. Modern psychology also emphasizes that self-awareness and emotional management are core abilities for personal growth and happiness.

Interpretation and Extension:

"He who knows contentment is rich; he who acts with determination has a strong will" points out that true wealth comes from inner contentment, and proper determination comes from steadfast actions. This saying teaches us that we can find inner strength and happiness through inner peace and adherence to our principles. We often neglect inner peace and contentment in modern society while pursuing external success and material wealth. In fact, only when we truly understand ourselves, manage our emotions, and stick to our beliefs can we find true peace and happiness in life.

Inner Strength

Inner strength is the foundation for facing various life challenges and difficulties. We can discover our inner potential and resilience by understanding and accepting ourselves. This strength not only helps us overcome external challenges but also allows us to remain calm and firm when facing internal conflicts and contradictions.

The Significance of Exploring Inner Strength

Many people neglect inner cultivation and self-understanding in their pursuit of external success. However, true wisdom and strength come from a deep understanding of oneself and inner peace. When we can delve into our inner selves and understand our emotions, thoughts, and motivations, we can confidently face various challenges in the external world. By perceiving our inner strength, we become more confident and resilient.

Inner strength is an indispensable part of our lives. Whether facing pressure, challenges, or changes, inner strength, and peace help us stay calm and make wise decisions. Inner strength includes emotional management, self-trust, and steadfast beliefs.

Research shows that individuals with strong inner strength can better cope with various stresses and challenges in life. They exhibit greater resilience and adaptability in the face of adversity. In his positive psychology theory, psychologist Martin Seligman points out that inner strength is crucial to well-being. Through self-reflection and positive thinking, we can enhance our inner strength and better deal with life's challenges (Seligman, 2011).

My Experience: Overcoming Inner Fears and Challenges

On my entrepreneurial journey, I have experienced many inner fears. When I resolutely resigned to start my own business, my parents were worried and opposed it. Transitioning from a familiar field of architectural design to a new domain, I had to face many new challenges and learn new skills. The pressure from the outside world and the inner conflicts formed a massive vortex in my mind, causing doubts and fears.

However, the wisdom of the Dao De Jing, "He who knows contentment is rich; he who acts with determination has a strong will," inspired me.

I learned to calm down and talk to myself when facing pressure and emotional agitation, listening to my inner voice to understand what I truly wanted. Sometimes, when my mind was too chaotic, I would take out paper and pen and write down all my thoughts. I would ask myself questions such as what I currently have and what I am afraid of. Then, I would write down or draw what I am good at, what I have, and my fears and worries, making them concrete and visual in front of me. When complex thoughts turned into specific drawings or words, everything no longer seemed so chaotic and illogical. I gradually felt the growth of inner strength.

I realized that this is actually a form of meditation: filtering out external noise through artistic creation to enhance focus. Using what I am good at to strengthen my inner self and overcome inner fears. When facing inner contradictions, I found inner strength and peace. Listening to my inner voice not only helped me overcome the initial difficulties of entrepreneurship but also made me more confident and calm when facing challenges. Through these experiences, I deeply understood that inner strength and peace are the foundation for facing various challenges and pressures in life.

Multisensory Art Meditation Practice

Please scan the QR to access the artwork for meditation practice.

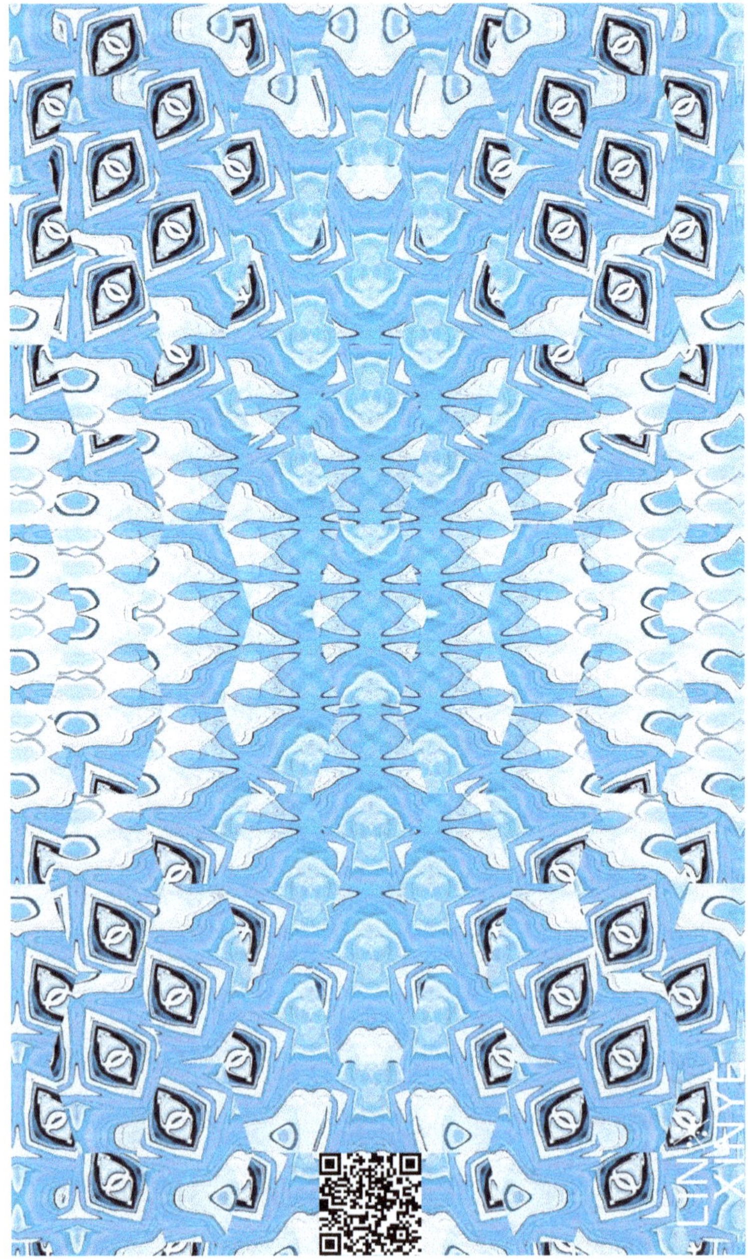

Viewing the artwork in the suggested feng shui direction for a better experience. A projector is recommended to display the artwork on a wall to create a more immersive meditation atmosphere.

Feng Shui Application: Enhancing Energy, Creating a Space for Inner Strength and Peace

Practice in the northern position of your meditation space to enhance the peaceful and harmonious energy of the space. Choose a quiet corner in your home as a meditation space, preferably in the north, as this direction is associated with calm and rational energy. Keep the space clean and tidy to reduce stress and anxiety. Placing small decorations such as lapis lazuli and clear quartz can enhance the energy flow in the space, further promoting inner peace and harmony. Use soft natural light or warm-toned lighting to create a cozy atmosphere. Soft blue and white decorations help create a peaceful and harmonious environment.

In the Wuxing - Five Elements theory, the north is associated with water, symbolizing wisdom and calmness. By combining the Five Elements theory, we can better utilize these natural elements and directional energies to enhance our overall well-being and inner peace.

For this week's multisensory art meditation, you could randomly select one or more of the following to practice together for unexpected benefits.

- Inner Garden Meditation: While appreciating the artwork, imagine yourself in a beautiful blue and white garden surrounded by blue flowers and plants. Feel the tranquility of the garden, spending a few minutes walking in this imagined garden and absorbing the peaceful energy around you.
- Sensory Connection: While appreciating the artwork, choose an object you like, such as a stone, a leaf, or a small sculpture. Touch the object, feeling its texture, shape, and temperature. This sensory connection can help you focus better and calm your mind.
- Aromatherapy: During meditation, light rosemary or neroli essential oil. Let the aroma fill the space, further relaxing your body and mind and enhancing the meditation effect.
- Crystal Use: During meditation, touch lapis lazuli and clear quartz, feeling their energy flow. This enhances the depth of meditation and emotional balance.

- Taste Integration: During appreciation and meditation, taste a piece of fresh mint leaf or mint candy . The refreshing and excellent taste can help you further relax your body and mind.

Colors Involved in the Artwork

- Blue: Represents calmness, trust, and wisdom, helping restore inner peace and harmony.

- White: Symbolizes purity, clarity, and new beginnings, helping clear negative emotions and enhance inner clarity.

Chakras Involved in the Artwork

- Throat Chakra (Vishuddha): Located at the center of the throat, associated with expression and communication. Meditation on the throat chakra can enhance our self-expression and inner sincerity.

- Crown Chakra (Sahasrara): Located at the top of the head, the crown chakra is associated with spiritual insight and higher consciousness. Meditation can help us connect to higher levels of consciousness, gaining inspiration and insight.

Recommended Essential Oils and Scents for the Artwork

- Rosemary: Refreshing and invigorating effects, helping relieve stress and enhance mood.

- Neroli: Soothing and relaxing effects, helping enhance inner peace and harmony.

Related Crystals

- Lapis Lazuli: Helps enhance the energy of the throat chakra, promoting self-expression and inner sincerity.

- Clear Quartz: Helps enhance the crown chakra's energy, promoting spirituality and emotional release.

Additionally, you can try these practices to continue strengthening your inner strength:

- Daily Reflection: Spend a few minutes each day recording your emotional changes and writing down events that triggered your emotions and reactions. You can better understand your emotional patterns and find ways to improve emotional management through reflection.

- Inner Dialogue: Have an inner dialogue with yourself, asking what you currently need and which emotions need attention and care. You can better understand your inner needs and enhance your self-understanding through inner dialogue.

- Creative Writing: Take a piece of paper and a pen and freely write down your feelings and thoughts. This unstructured writing can help you release inner emotions and find inner balance.

Creating Time: Art Creation for Inner Strength

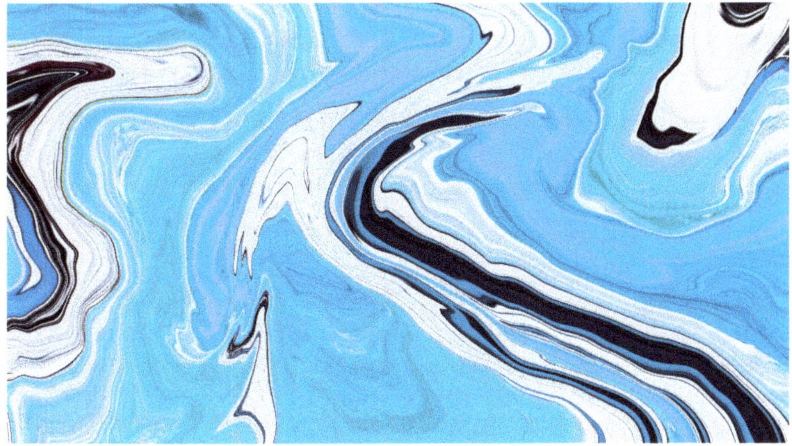

Let's practice a comprehensive exercise to review and master multisensory art meditation. This meditation exercise helps you enhance your inner strength and inspires you to explore your own creative meditation method.

Steps:

- Prepare Materials: Gather a blank sheet of paper and a variety of colorful art tools that inspire you, such as colored pencils, markers, or pastels. Feel free to include additional creative elements like textured paper or found objects.

- Enter Meditation State: Sit comfortably in your chosen space. Close your eyes, take a few deep breaths, and allow all your muscles to relax. Imagine yourself surrounded by a pure white bright light, feeling its warmth and clarity enveloping you.

- Start Creating: Open your eyes and draw the emerging emotions and inspirations. Let your creativity flow freely, without judgment. Create abstract patterns, vivid scenes, or anything that resonates with your inner state. Focus on your emotional expression and enjoy the process.

- Aromatherapy: To enhance your creative experience by applying aroma, light rosemary or neroli essential oil is recommended for this practice. Allow the soothing aroma to permeate your space, promoting relaxation and deepening your meditative state.

- Crystal Use: Hold lapis lazuli and clear quartz during meditation and creative process. Feel their energies enhance your meditation, promote emotional balance, and deepen your connection to your inner self.

- Taste Integration: Try tasting a slice of juicy orange. Focus on the sensory experience, feeling the burst of citrus flavor and the refreshing sweetness, allowing it to invigorate and rejuvenate your senses.

- End and Record Experience: Take a moment to appreciate your creation quietly. Reflect on your feelings and experiences during the process. Write down your observations, noting any changes in your energy and the sense of relaxation and creativity you've achieved.

Interactive Questions and Reflections

- How can you discern and listen to your inner voice amidst daily chaos? What practices can help you strengthen this ability?
- In what ways have you noticed inner peace contributing to your resilience and decision-making during challenging times?
- How could you incorporate the principles of contentment and determination into your daily life to enhance your inner strength and emotional well-being?

Document your reflections in a personal notebook. Take time to review them. Sharing your thoughts and art creations with the group is highly recommended to enhance the experience.

Meet, share, and grow with creative spirits globally.
(Group QR code is located in p37)

....

References

- Seligman, M. E. P. (2011). Flourish: A Visionary New Understanding of Happiness and Well-being.
- APA. (2020). Stress in America™ 2020: A National Mental Health Crisis.

CHAPTER IV
EMOTIONAL MANAGEMENT

ENHANCING HAPPINESS

Have you ever noticed how these emotions affect your life and decision-making when facing emotional fluctuations and stress? How do you regulate and manage your emotions to enhance your happiness?

> He who conquers others is strong; he who conquers himself is mighty.
>
> — Dao De Jing, Chapter 33

This ancient wisdom from the Dao De Jing teaches us to value self-control and inner strength. The wisdom of the Dao De Jing tells us that conquering others requires strength, but conquering oneself requires even greater inner power. This means that we can only truly achieve inner strength and stability when we can control and manage our emotions. This inner power and peace are key to emotional management and enhancing happiness. Modern psychology also emphasizes that self-control and emotional management are core personal growth and happiness capabilities.

Interpretation and Extension:

"He who conquers others is strong; he who conquers himself is mighty" highlights that true strength comes from inner control and self-management. When we can conquer our emotions and control our inner world, we can achieve true peace and happiness. In modern society, we often experience emotional fluctuations due to external pressures and challenges, but we can only find inner peace and harmony through inner self-management and emotional control.

This wisdom aligns with modern psychological research. Psychologist Daniel Goleman, in his emotional intelligence theory, points out that emotional management is vital to emotional intelligence. Through meditation and self-reflection, we can enhance our ability to manage emotions, making wiser choices when facing difficulties (Goleman, 1995).

Exploring the Importance of Emotional Management

Emotions are an unavoidable part of our lives. Joy, anger, sadness, or fear influence our daily lives to varying degrees. When emotions crash over us like waves, we must learn to observe and accept them like rocks on the shore rather than being swept away. Emotional management refers to our ability to recognize, regulate, and control our emotions. By understanding and accepting our emotions, we can better cope with life's pressures and challenges, finding inner peace and harmony.

Research shows that we struggle to make correct decisions when driven by emotions. Daniel Goleman's theory of emotional intelligence suggests that managing emotions is crucial for emotional intelligence. Through meditation and self-reflection, we can enhance our ability to manage emotions and make wiser decisions when facing difficulties (Goleman, 1995). Meditation teaches us to master our emotions rather than being controlled by them.

How Multisensory Art Meditation Influences Emotional Management and Happiness

A Harvard Medical School study shows that individuals engaged in art creation and appreciation significantly improve their emotional management and happiness. The study found that art activities help people more effectively process emotional stress, reduce anxiety and depression symptoms, and significantly enhance overall mental health and happiness (Harvard Health Publishing, 2018). Regular multisensory art meditation practice can strengthen brain areas related to emotion regulation, promoting positive emotions and reducing negative ones. An Oxford University study found that adults participating in art activities had significantly higher emotional stability and life satisfaction than the control group (Oxford University, 2017).

In multisensory art meditation practice, appreciating multisensory meditation artworks can provide emotional support, enhancing emotional management and happiness. Understanding and accepting one's emotions is also crucial.

Multisensory art meditation offers a safe channel for emotional expression through painting, sculpture, or other forms of art creation, allowing us to externalize and release inner emotions.

Additionally, multisensory practices stimulate our senses comprehensively, enriching our perceptual experiences and helping us better understand our emotional responses, enhancing self-awareness and achieving emotional balance and harmony more effectively.

My Experience: Managing Emotions Through Multisensory Art

After I chose to start my own business, my mindset underwent significant changes. Previously, with a job, I had a stable income and life security each month. I only needed to complete assigned tasks on time daily without worrying about much. However, everything changed after resigning. I had to take responsibility for myself, making reasonable plans with limited funds to ensure everything ran smoothly. Under enormous pressure, I often experienced emotional fluctuations. These emotions were often negative; these emotions broke me down mentally and disabled me from working on anything. Unintentionally, I would vent my emotions on loved ones, causing unnecessary conflicts and arguments and hurting those I love.

As an artist, emotional fluctuations once made me desire expression and inspiration. However, ever since I became an entrepreneur without a sense of security, it has been no longer an inspiration. These emotions hurt me in many ways, and I needed to handle my emotions rationally to ensure my plans could be executed and my decision could be made logistically. I gradually found my solution by addressing these emotions through creation. When I freely expressed my inner feelings in multisensory art creation and meditation, I gradually learned to self-control and manage, soothe my mood, and improve my emotion management.

Multisensory Art Meditation Practice

Please scan the QR to access the artwork for meditation practice.

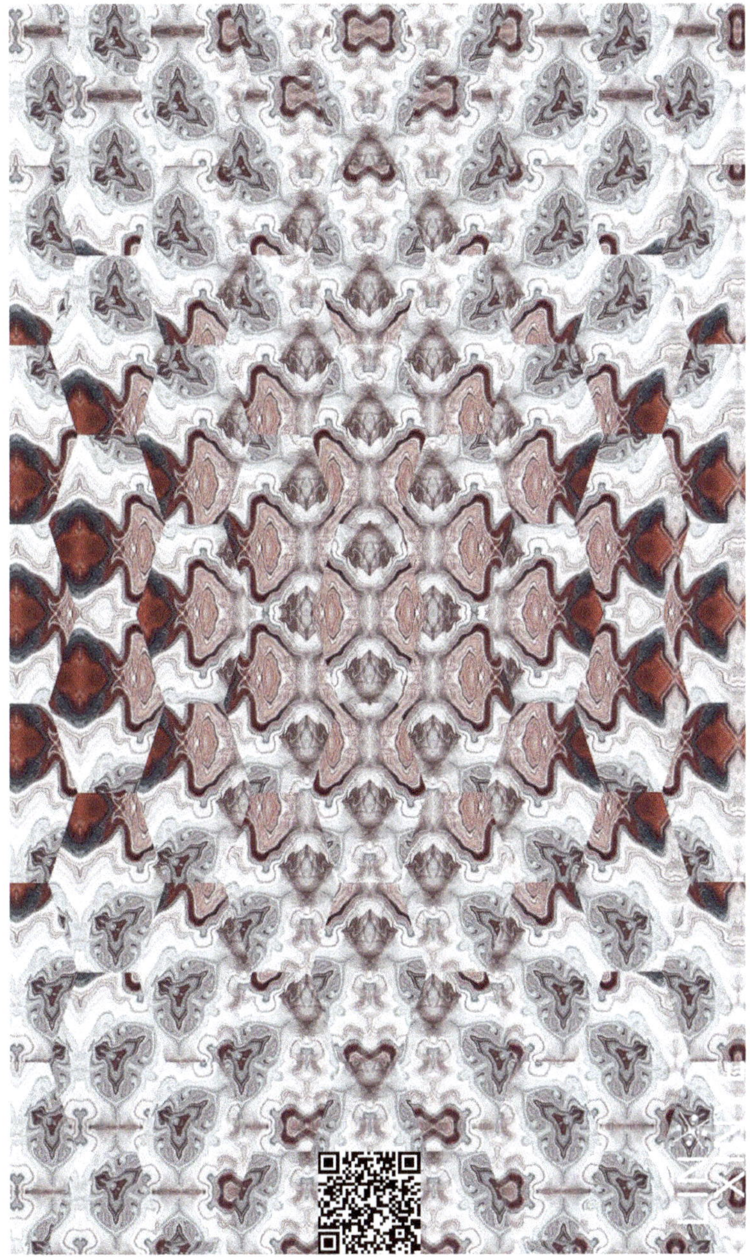

Viewing the artwork in the suggested feng shui direction for a better experience. A projector is recommended to display the artwork on a wall to create a more immersive meditation atmosphere.

Feng Shui Application: Enhancing Energy and Creating a Balanced Emotional Space

Practice in the southeast or northwest of your meditation space to enhance the space's harmony and stability. Choose a quiet corner at home as your meditation space, preferably in the southeast or northwest, as these directions are linked to health and balanced energies. Keep the space clean and tidy to reduce stress and anxiety. Place small decorations like amethyst and rose quartz to enhance the natural energy of the space. Use soft natural light or warm-toned lighting to create a cozy atmosphere. Decorating with soft, neutral colors helps create a calm and peaceful environment.

In the Wuxing - Five Elements theory, the southeast belongs to wood, representing growth and balance, while the northwest belongs to metal, representing clarity and purity. These Feng Shui principles can bring more peace and stability to your meditation space.

For this week's multisensory art meditation, you could randomly select one or more of the following to practice together for unexpected benefits.

- Emotion Identification: While viewing the artwork, identify your current emotions. Accept and acknowledge their presence, whether joy, sadness, anger, or calm.

- Deep Breathing: Find a quiet place to sit and practice deep breathing while listening to the artwork's music. Inhale through your nose, feeling your abdomen rise, then slowly exhale through your mouth, feeling your abdomen fall. Repeat this process for a few minutes until you feel calm inside.

- Incorporating Scents: During meditation, light ylang-ylang or cedarwood essential oils. Let the scent fill the space, further relaxing your body and mind and enhancing the meditation effect.

- Taste Combination: Before and after viewing and meditating, enjoy a small cup of warm cinnamon tea. Feel its warmth and layers of flavor, further relaxing your body and mind. (If you don't like cinnamon tea, replace it with any other tea you prefer.)

- Sensory Connection: While viewing the artwork, choose to touch a soft or relaxed object. Feel its texture, shape, and temperature. Through tactile connection, you can better focus and calm your mind.

Colors Involved in the Artwork

- Red: Represents vitality, passion, and strength, helping to enhance emotions and energy.

- Brown: Symbolizes stability, reliability, and security, helping to relieve stress and promote inner peace.

- Gray: Represents balance, calm, and neutrality, helping to calm emotions.

- Light Gray: Symbolizes purity, peace, and freshness, helping to enhance inner calm.

Chakras Involved in the Artwork

- Crown Chakra (Sahasrara): Located at the top of the head, associated with spiritual enlightenment and higher consciousness. Through Crown Chakra meditation, we can connect with higher levels of consciousness, gaining inspiration and enlightenment and enhancing happiness.

- Root Chakra (Muladhara): Located at the base of the spine, associated with survival and basic security. Through Root Chakra meditation, we can enhance our inner stability, help manage emotions, and promote inner peace.

Recommended Essential Oils and Scents for the Artwork

- Ylang-Ylang: Relaxing and soothing effects, helping to enhance emotional balance and happiness.

- Cedarwood: Refreshing and uplifting effects, helping to relieve stress and enhance emotions.

Related Crystals

- Red Agate: Helps enhance the energy of the root chakra, promoting confidence and personal strength. Red agate corresponds to the earth element, enhancing our inner stability and basic security.

- Moonstone: This gemstone enhances the energy of the crown chakra, promoting spiritual insight and emotional balance. It corresponds to the metal element, facilitating our connection to inspiration and higher consciousness.

You can also incorporate these practices to strengthen emotional management further:

- Mindfulness Meditation: Continue deep breathing, focusing on the present moment. Do not judge your thoughts and emotions; observe and accept them. This mindfulness meditation can help you better perceive and regulate your emotions.

- Brief Creation: If time allows, pick up a piece of paper and some colored pencils or crayons and freely draw your current feelings. This brief creation can help you externalize emotions, achieving inner balance and relief.

- Emotion Journal: Record your emotional changes, noting events that trigger emotions and your reactions. This will help you better understand your emotional patterns and find ways to improve emotional management.

Creating Time: Art Creation for Unleashing Potential

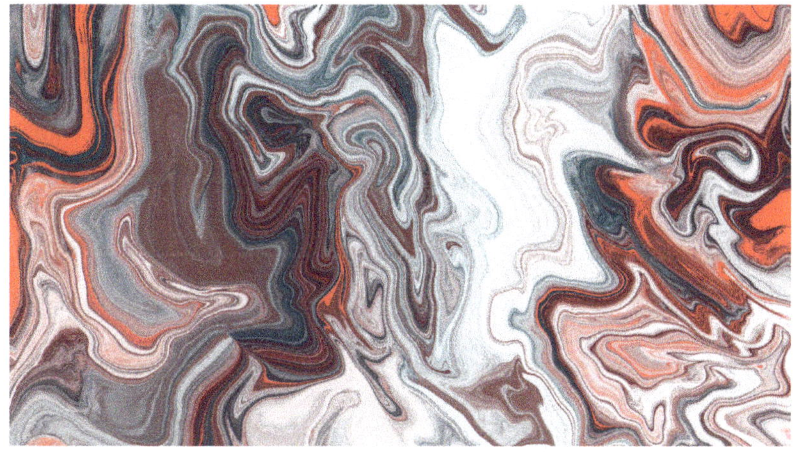

Let's practice a comprehensive exercise to review and master multisensory art meditation. This exercise is a meditation practice and helps you manage emotions and create your meditative artwork.

Steps:

- Prepare Materials: A sheet of white paper and several colored pens or pencils. These tools will help you express your emotions visually.

- Create a Calming Space: Choose a quiet and comfortable corner at home, preferably in the southeast or northwest direction, as these areas are associated with health and balanced energy in Feng Shui. Ensure the space is clean and free of clutter. Enhance the space's energy by placing small decorations like amethyst and rose quartz.

- Enter Meditation State: Sit in the chosen space, take a few deep breaths, and consciously relax all your muscles. Close your eyes and imagine your emotions as a tranquil pond. Observe the pond's surface—notice if it's calm or if there are ripples. Each breath out is like a breeze gently smoothing the surface, releasing any emotional tension. Allow yourself to feel lighter and more at peace with each breath.

- Start Creating: Open your eyes and let your hands flow freely with the colored pens or pencils, channeling your emotions onto the paper. Imagine your emotions as colors, shapes, and lines—fiery reds and sharp angles for anger, soothing blues and gentle curves for calm, vibrant yellows, and dynamic spirals for joy. Allow your feelings to dictate the movement of your hand, creating an abstract symphony of your inner world. Don't worry about the final product; immerse yourself in the expressive journey and the cathartic release it brings.

- Incorporate Scents: Light ylang-ylang or cedarwood essential oil during your creation. Allow the soothing scent to permeate the space, further relaxing your body and mind and enhancing the meditation experience.

- Use Crystals: During meditation and creation, touch red agate and moonstone. Feel their calming and balancing energies flowing through you, deepening your meditation and promoting emotional balance.

- Taste Integration: Slowly savor a spoonful of honey, noting how it melts in your mouth and its natural sweetness and warmth. This mindful tasting can bring comfort and relaxation, grounding your senses.

- Conclude and Record Experiences: After completing your drawing, take a moment to appreciate your work quietly. Reflect on your emotional journey during the process. Record your feelings and experiences, noting any changes in the energy of your surroundings and your emotional state. This reflection can help solidify the emotional balance and creative inspiration you've gained.

Interactive Questions and Reflections

- How do you cope with emotional fluctuations and pressure in daily life? What new methods can you try to enhance your emotional management and happiness?
- How do you think emotional management helps your sensory acuity and creativity?
- How do you use meditation and art creation to maintain inner peace and harmony when facing external pressures and internal tensions?

Document your reflections in a personal notebook. Take time to review them. Sharing your thoughts and art creations with the group is highly recommended to enhance the experience.

Meet, share, and grow with creative spirits globally.

(Group QR code is located in p37)

....

References

- Goleman, D. (1995). Emotional Intelligence.
- Harvard Health Publishing. (2018). The Healing Power of Art.
- Oxford University. (2017). Arts and Mental Wellbeing.

CHAPTER V
IMAGINATION AND CREATIVITY

CULTIVATING AND STIMULATING

Have you ever tried combining knowledge and experiences from different fields to create new ideas and innovations? What have you gained from this endeavor?

> The movement of the Dao is reversal; the method of
> the Dao is yielding.
> — Dao De Jing, Chapter 40

This wisdom from Dao De Jing reveals the workings of the Dao, where reversal and yielding are key. It suggests that the development of things often occurs through opposition and transformation and that what seems weak often holds great power. This seemingly paradoxical phenomenon contains profound natural laws and wisdom.

Interpretation and Extension:

"The movement of the Dao is reversal" indicates that the development and change of things are often achieved through the mutual transformation of opposites. For example, the end of the day means the arrival of night, and the passing of winter brings the beginning of spring. This way of reverse movement is a common rule in nature and a manifestation of innovative thinking. When facing difficulties and challenges, we should act contrary to expectations, breaking conventional thinking patterns and sparking more creative ideas and solutions.

"The method of the Dao is yielding" emphasizes the importance of softness and flexibility in nature. Seemingly weak things often possess enduring vitality and boundless potential.

The power of water lies in its flexibility and inclusiveness, enabling it to penetrate rocks and nourish all living things. For imagination and creativity, this quality of softness is equally essential. A flexible mindset and an open heart can accommodate more possibilities, nurturing innovative ideas and unique solutions.

The Magical Power of Imagination and Creativity

Imagination and creativity are the core forces driving the continuous progress of human civilization. Imagination allows us to transcend existing cognitive frameworks and explore unknown territories, while creativity enables us to turn these novel ideas into concrete solutions and innovative outcomes. Whether scientific breakthroughs, technological advancements, or artistic prosperity, imagination and creativity play crucial roles. They not only drive the overall progress of society but also profoundly influence personal growth and success. Cultivating these two abilities might bring surprises to your life.

Research also shows that people with rich imaginations exhibit stronger adaptability and innovation when facing new challenges and environments. Imagination stimulates us to keep learning and exploring, while creativity helps us apply acquired knowledge to real problems and find innovative solutions. Psychologist Carol Dweck's Growth Mindset theory points out that imagination and creativity are important drivers for continuous learning and growth (Dweck, 2006).

How Multisensory Art Meditation Stimulates the Brain's Imagination and Creativity

Multisensory art meditation, which combines visual, auditory, and tactile stimuli, helps to stimulate the brain's imagination and creativity. Neuroscientific research suggests that such multisensory stimulation can enhance connectivity between different brain regions, improving attention and cognitive flexibility and promoting creative thinking development. Through multisensory art meditation, the brain's default mode network (DMN), which is closely related to innovative thinking and the generation of inspiration, can be activated.

Multisensory art meditation is not just a simple relaxation exercise; it integrates multiple sensory experiences to help us enter a deeper state of meditation and stimulate latent creativity.

A study by Stanford University found that individuals participating in multisensory art meditation performed significantly better in creative thinking tests than the control group (Stanford University, 2020).

This practice guides us to focus on various sensory experiences, such as viewing art, listening to music or natural sounds, and touching different textures. It helps us fully stimulate the brain's potential. Through this method, we can not only improve our own imagination and creativity but also better apply these skills in daily life, finding innovative solutions and new sources of inspiration.

My Experience: A Journey of Exploration and Creation

Imagination and creativity have always been my secret weapons throughout my artistic creation and entrepreneurship journey, bringing limitless possibilities and providing direction and motivation for learning and experimenting. This also requires gratitude for a habit I cherish—continuous meditation, creation, and documentation. When facing countless unknown challenges and feeling a lack of inspiration, I open my notebook filled with abstract feelings and fleeting ideas I have recorded. They gradually develop into exciting projects by freely combining and associating this information. Imagination and creativity help generate new ideas in work and life and aid in excavating and activating the accumulated knowledge in familiar fields. I have combined my ideas with continuous practice to form my artistic style and entrepreneurial concepts. I can now write this book to reflect on and share these valuable insights.

Personal growth background, inner experiences, expertise, and life experiences are the best sources of inspiration. These are the unique treasures each person possesses. However, most of us leave little space for ourselves, gradually overlooking the treasures hidden within our bodies, forgetting how to activate and connect them to maximize their value. Through consistent practice of multisensory art and meditation, you can reignite your thinking and reactivate your potential.

Multisensory Art Meditation Practice

Please scan the QR to access the artwork for meditation practice.

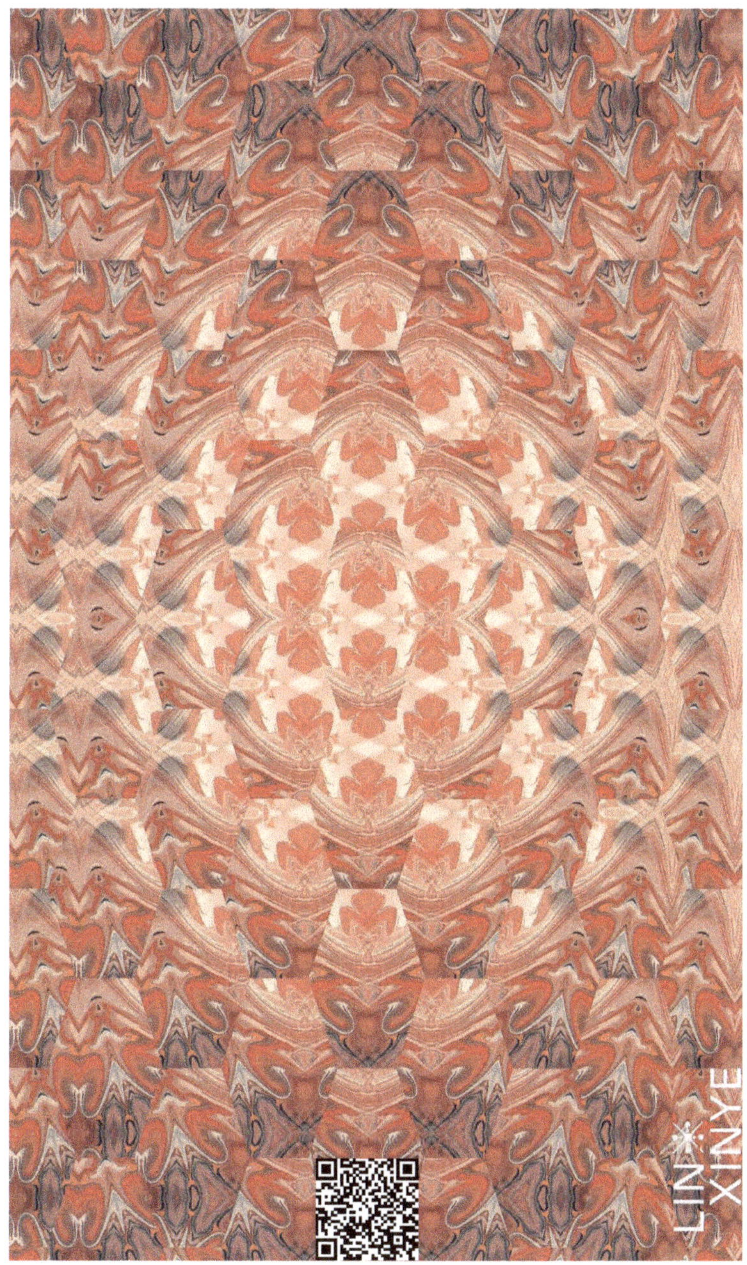

Viewing the artwork in the suggested feng shui direction for a better experience. A projector is recommended to display the artwork on a wall to create a more immersive meditation atmosphere.

Feng Shui Application: Enhancing Energy, Stimulating Imagination and Creativity in Your Space

The east symbolizes renewal and vitality. Placing art in this direction can infuse your creative and meditative processes with the inspiration of the morning light. Choose a corner filled with natural light, preferably in the eastern direction, as it is associated with the energy of renewal and vitality. Keep the space clean and tidy to enhance clarity of thought and creativity.

In the Wuxing - Five Elements theory, the east belongs to wood, representing growth and vitality. Placing green plants or wooden furniture in the eastern position can further enhance the energy of growth and creativity. Applying these Feng Shui principles can bring more creativity and inspiration to your meditation space.

For this week's multisensory art meditation, you could randomly select one or more of the following to practice together for unexpected benefits.

- Fantasy Adventure: While viewing the artwork, imagine yourself entering a mysterious world of these colors. Describe the surrounding scenes, sounds, and smells in as much detail as possible. Imagine what you discover and the adventures you experience in this new environment. This fantasy can stimulate your creativity and curiosity.

- Sensory Collage: While viewing the artwork, prepare materials with different textures, such as fabric, paper, leaves, etc. Touch these materials and feel their textures and temperatures. Then, collage them on paper to create a unique sensory collage. This process can stimulate creativity and help you discover new inspiration through sensory exploration.

- Incorporate Scents: During meditation, light ginger or rosemary essential oil. Let the scent permeate the space, enhancing your sensory experience and deepening the meditation effect.

- Use Crystals: Touch yellow citrine, orange agate, and red agate and feel their energy flow. This will enhance the depth of meditation and stimulate creativity.

- Taste Integration: Treat yourself to a small piece of creamy brie cheese paired with a slice of ripe pear. Focus on the smooth, rich texture of the cheese and the sweet juiciness of the pear, allowing this delightful combination to enhance your sense of accomplishment and relaxation.

Colors Involved in the Artwork

- Yellow: Represents vitality, innovation, and wisdom, helping to stimulate creativity and new thinking.

- Orange: Symbolizes vitality, warmth, and optimism, helping to enhance inner creativity and inspiration.

- Red: Represents passion, energy, and action, helping to stimulate creativity and new thinking.

- Blue: Symbolizes depth, wisdom, and calmness, helping to stimulate inner insight and creativity.

- Gray: Represents balance, calmness, and neutrality, helping to create a peaceful, creative environment.

Chakras Involved in the Artwork

- Solar Plexus Chakra: Located in the center of the abdomen, the solar plexus chakra is associated with confidence and personal power. Meditating on it can enhance our confidence and creativity.

- Sacral Chakra: Located below the navel, associated with emotions and desires. Meditating on the sacral chakra can help us stimulate inner inspiration and innovative thinking.

- Root Chakra: Located at the base of the spine, associated with survival and security. Meditating on the root chakra can enhance our stability and creativity.

Recommended Essential Oils and Scents for the Artwork

- Ginger: Has a warm and stimulating effect, helping to enhance concentration and stimulate imagination.

- Rosemary: Has a soothing and refreshing effect, helping to enhance inner calmness and creativity.

Related Crystals

- Yellow Citrine: Helps enhance the energy of the solar plexus chakra, promoting confidence and personal power.

- Orange Agate: Helps enhance the energy of the sacral chakra, enhancing inspiration and intuition.

- Red Agate: Helps enhance the root chakra's energy, promoting stability and personal power.

You can also incorporate these practices to develop your creativity and imagination further:

- Inspiration Capture: Carry a small notebook to record interesting things you encounter, sudden inspirations, or whimsical ideas. Whether it's an interesting conversation, a moving piece of music, or a beautiful scene, these can all be sources of your creativity. Regularly review these notes; you will find many new ideas and inspirations.

o   Sound Doodle: Randomly choose a piece of music you have never heard before and doodle freely on paper, following the rhythm of the music. Let the changes and rhythms of the music guide your strokes, and see what patterns and shapes you can create. This combination of sound and vision can stimulate your creativity and allow you to experience music and art in a new way.

o   Dream Diary: Record the scenes and stories you experience in your dreams after viewing and meditating. Dreams are often filled with whimsical ideas and are not constrained by reality's logic, making them a valuable resource for stimulating creativity. Recording and analyzing your dreams can give you many unique ideas and inspirations.

o   Creative Association Game: Choose two seemingly unrelated objects or concepts and try to link them together to create a new story or object. For example, imagine the combination of "ice cream" and "spaceship." What would it look like? This association game can train your thinking flexibility and stimulate creativity.

Creating Time: The Art of Imagination and Creativity

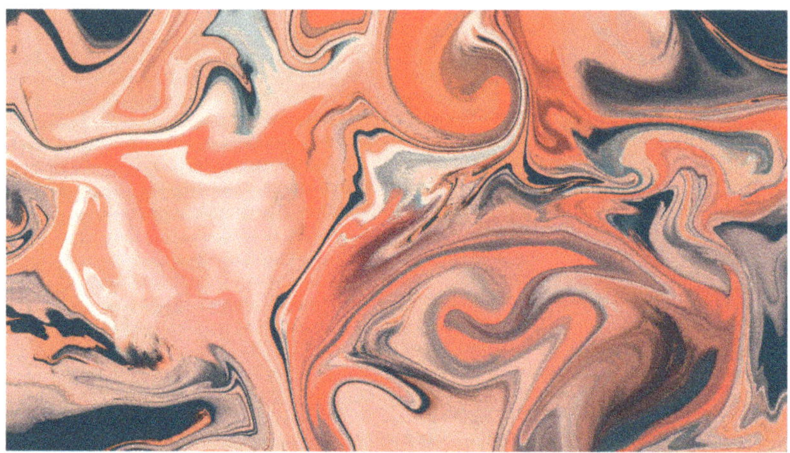

Now, let's review and master multisensory art meditation through a comprehensive exercise. This practice is a meditation exercise and helps stimulate imagination and creativity, allowing you to create your own meditation art.

Steps:

- Start Creating: Use the scissors and colored paper to cut shapes, patterns, or symbols that match your current emotions and inspirations. Glue these paper cuttings onto the white paper to create a unique collage. Focus on your feelings and emotional expressions during the creation process. Don't worry about the outcome; enjoy the process.

- Incorporate Scents: During creation, use light orange blossom or rosemary essential oil to let the scent permeate the space, enhancing your sensory experience and deepening the meditation effect.

- Activate Multiple Senses: Enhance your creative process by incorporating the following multisensory elements:

- Touch: Integrate textured materials into your collage. Attach fabric, leaves, or paper scraps to create a tactile art piece.

- Sound: Play instrumental music that inspires you, letting the rhythm and melody influence your artistic expression.

- Use Crystals: During meditation and creation, touch yellow citrine, orange agate, and red agate. Feel their energy flow, enhancing the depth of meditation and stimulating creativity.

- Taste Integration: Sprinkle a small amount of salt on mango slices. Combining sweet and salty stimulates the taste buds and the brain's creative thinking, helping you spark inspiration and creativity in daily life.

- Conclude and Record Experiences: After completing the collage, quietly appreciate your work and record your feelings and experiences in the notebook. Note the energy changes in the surrounding environment and feel the enhancement of imagination and creativity. Reflect on the creative journey you experienced during the process and any new ideas or insights that emerged.

Interactive Questions and Reflections

- How do you maintain your imagination and innovation spirit in daily life? What new methods can you try to stimulate your creativity?
- How do you think imagination and creativity help your personal growth and career development?
- How do you use meditation and artistic creation to stimulate your imagination and creativity when facing new challenges and opportunities?

Document your reflections in a personal notebook. Take time to review them. Sharing your thoughts and art creations with the group is highly recommended to enhance the experience.

Meet, share, and grow with creative spirits globally.
(Group QR code is located in p37)

....

References
- Dweck, C. S. (2006). Mindset: The new psychology of success. Random House. Goleman, D. (1995).
- Emotional Intelligence: Why it can matter more than IQ. Bantam Books. Harvard Health Publishing. (2018).
- The healing power of art. Harvard Health. Oxford University. (2017).
- Arts and mental wellbeing. Oxford University Press. Stanford University. (2020).
- Multisensory meditation and creativity. Stanford University Press.

CHAPTER VI
SELF–ACCEPTANCE AND SELF–LOVE

ACHIEVING INNER HARMONY

When was the last time you felt genuinely satisfied with yourself? How did you acknowledge and appreciate that moment?

> Being compassionate brings courage.
> — Dao De Jing, Chapter 67

This wisdom reveals the intrinsic connection between compassion and courage. We find inner strength and bravery by treating ourselves and others with compassion. This mindset is crucial for self-acceptance and self-love. Embracing and loving ourselves leads to inner peace and harmony, enhancing our overall quality of life and happiness.

Interpretation and Extension:

"Being compassionate brings courage" suggests that true courage stems from deep compassion. When we treat ourselves and others with kindness, inner strength naturally emerges. For instance, when we accept our flaws and imperfections, our internal pressure decreases, making us more confident and brave. This compassion is not only about caring for others but also about being gentle and understanding with ourselves.

The courage born from compassion is not just emotional support but a profound inner strength. Being compassionate towards ourselves can build a strong inner self, boosting our confidence and self-esteem. This courage helps us remain calm and composed when facing challenges, finding inner harmony and peace.

In the journey of self-acceptance and self-love, compassion is key. Being kind to ourselves means accepting our strengths and weaknesses and embracing our imperfections. This attitude helps us build a healthy self-image, enhancing our inner peace and happiness.

Therefore, "Being compassionate brings courage" is not only a life wisdom but also a way of living. By treating ourselves with compassion, we can achieve inner harmony and balance, improving our overall quality of life and happiness.

The Power of Self-Acceptance and Self-Love

In pursuing external recognition and success, we often neglect self-care, falling into the trap of self-criticism. However, self-acceptance and self-love are the cornerstones of mental health and happiness, helping us find inner peace and strength.

Self-Acceptance:

Self-acceptance means unconditionally accepting oneself, including all strengths and weaknesses. This involves acknowledging our strengths and facing and embracing our flaws. When we honestly face our imperfections, internal conflicts, and pressure decrease, leading to true peace. This peace is not about escaping reality but courageously facing ourselves and accepting our uniqueness.

Imagine facing a daunting task filled with self-doubt and anxiety. You might repeatedly ask yourself, "Can I do this? Am I good enough?" These questions plant seeds of insecurity, causing you to lose direction under pressure. But if you learn self-acceptance, you will say, "I have done my best. I deserve love." This attitude relieves stress and allows you to face challenges positively.

Psychological research shows that self-acceptance is closely related to mental health, significantly enhancing self-esteem and confidence while reducing anxiety and depression (Neff, 2011).

Self-Love:

Self-love is a deep respect for oneself. It allows us to take care of our physical and mental health, thereby improving overall happiness. Through self-love, we build a strong inner self, increasing confidence and self-esteem. It enables us to remain calm and composed when facing life's challenges. Self-love is not selfishness but healthy self-attention.

Psychologist Kristin Neff's theory of "Self-Compassion" indicates that self-acceptance and self-love help us become more resilient in the face of setbacks, reducing anxiety and depression and enhancing overall happiness (Neff, 2003).

Achieving Inner Harmony:

Self-acceptance and self-love help us cope with life's challenges and significantly enhance mental health and happiness. Through inner harmony, we can remain calm and steadfast amidst external turmoil. Everyone has qualities worthy of love and should learn to love themselves. Through self-acceptance and self-love, we find inner balance and harmony, improving overall life quality and happiness.

My Experience: From Perfectionism to Self-Acceptance and Self-Love

I have always been a perfectionist, constantly frustrated by my inability to achieve perfection in life and creation. When results did not meet expectations, I would fall into deep self-reproach. My perfectionism made me dislike my imperfections. No matter what I did, a sharp inner voice would critically judge everything. Especially during the most challenging times of my failed entrepreneurship, I lived in depression and self-blame every day. This inner criticism and harsh judgment made it difficult for me to enjoy anything, accumulating much negative energy fully. This negativity spread within me and overflowed, hurting those who cared about me. I still often struggle with this inner critic. Whenever I fall short, that voice reappears, criticizing me and making me dislike myself.

It took me a long time to realize that our hearts are like a fragile child. I had never truly loved myself, especially during failure and low points. I locked that fragile child in a dark room, trying to ignore her. When she cried, I couldn't love myself, those around me, or the world. After many setbacks and hardships, I understood I spent too much time seeking external validation and forgot to recognize myself. Many people chase love from others but forget they also have the power to give themselves much love.

I remember a moment before a crucial exhibition when I broke down. Standing in the middle of my studio, looking at the countless revised yet unsatisfactory works, I felt helpless and desperate. I cried a lot as if releasing all the pressure and pain. At that moment, I realized that I must learn to be kind to myself and accept my imperfections, or I will be consumed by my own harshness.

I started smiling at myself in the mirror every day. No matter how bad things got, I forced myself to say a few words of praise. I decided to be kind to that fragile child inside, accepting her imperfections. This is a slow reconciliation process, and it is still ongoing. Although the process continues, I can already feel the harmony and happiness within me gradually growing.

This is a long journey, requiring constantly breaking the ingrained thinking patterns in your mind. You need to combat that harsh, critical voice in your head consciously. When it starts saying hurtful words, you must immediately correct it, using a gentler, more grateful, and loving approach to dialogue with your heart. Only by being kind and cherishing yourself can you begin to feel the love within, and then you can transmit that love, loving others. When love flows, you will feel everything starting to shine.

Although this is my most vulnerable side, I decided to reveal it because I know many people have had similar experiences. Through this honest sharing, I hope to remind those still in some life vortex that you can accept and love yourself, finding inner peace and harmony.

Multisensory Art Meditation Practice

Please scan the QR to access the artwork for meditation practice.

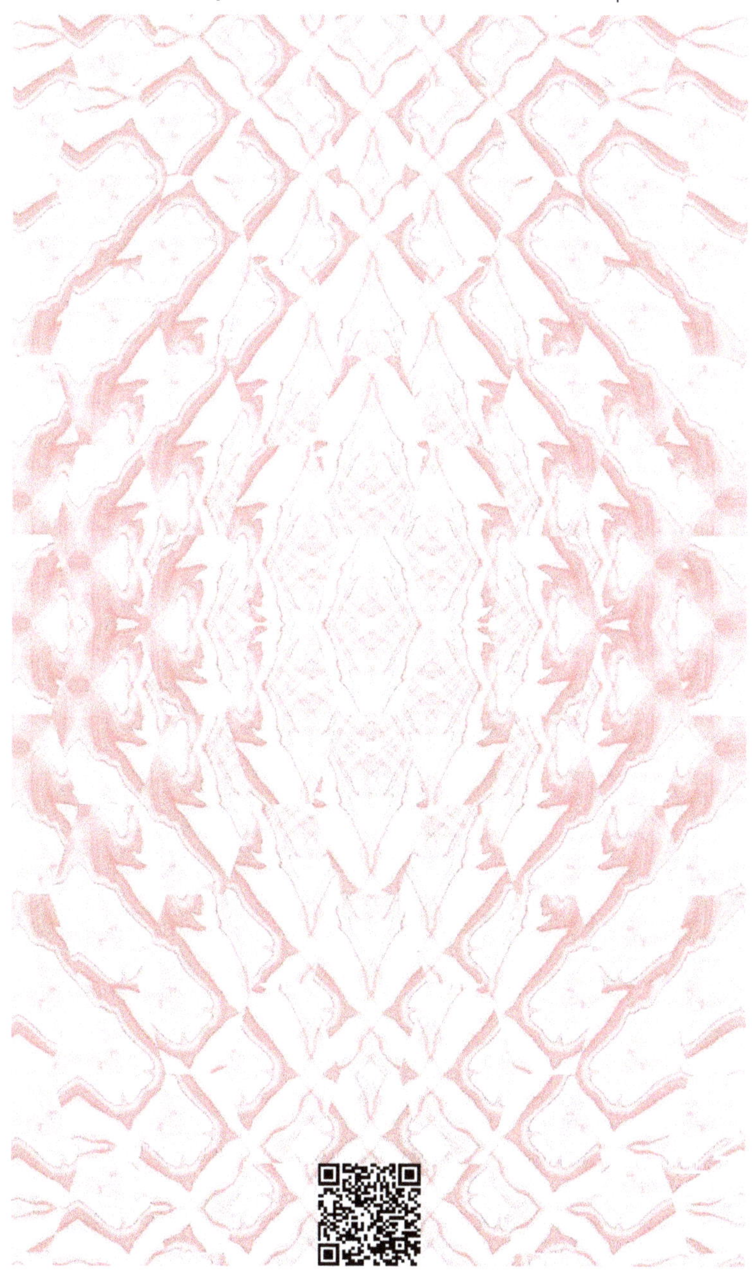

Viewing the artwork in the suggested feng shui direction for a better experience. A projector is recommended to display the artwork on a wall to create a more immersive meditation atmosphere.

Feng Shui Application: Enhancing Energy and Creating a Space for SelfAcceptance and Self-Love

The east symbolizes renewal and vitality. Hanging "Self-Acceptance and Self-Love" in your meditation space's eastern position can enhance the space's warmth and harmony. Choose a corner of your home filled with natural light as a meditation space, preferably facing east, as this direction is associated with the energy of renewal and vitality. Keep the space clean and tidy to enhance clarity of thought and inner peace.

In the Wuxing - Five Elements theory, the east corresponds to wood, representing growth and vitality. Placing flowers or green plants in the eastern position can further enhance the energy of growth and harmony. These Feng Shui principles can bring more warmth and self-love to your meditation space. Use bright natural light or warm lighting to create a cozy atmosphere. Warm-colored decorations can help create an environment of warmth and love, aiding in finding inner peace and harmony during meditation.

For this week's multisensory art meditation, you could randomly select one or more of the following to practice together for unexpected benefits.

- Daily Affirmations: While viewing the work, say three positive affirmations to yourself, such as "I accept and love myself," "I believe in my abilities," "I deserve happiness." This affirmation can enhance your confidence and self-esteem.
- Incorporate Scents: During viewing and meditation, light rose, or sandalwood essential oil lets the scent fill the space, enhancing the sensory experience and meditation effect.
- Emotional Release: While viewing the work, recall a recent experience of feeling frustrated or failing. Allow yourself to feel these emotions, then imagine these negative emotions being released with your breath through deep breathing.
- Using Crystals: While viewing the work and practicing, touch rose quartz and yellow jade, feeling their energy flow. This enhances the depth of meditation and the power of self-acceptance.

- Taste Integration: After meditation and creation, enjoy a small bowl of yogurt, experiencing the taste stimulation it brings and feeling inner peace and joy.

Colors Involved in the Artwork

- Pink: Represents gentleness, love, and care, helping to stimulate self-acceptance and love.

- Ivory: Symbolizes purity, peace, and tranquility, helping to enhance inner peace and happiness.

Chakras Involved in the Artwork

- Heart Chakra: Located in the center of the chest, the heart chakra is associated with love and emotions. Meditating on the heart chakra can enhance emotional expression and acceptance.

- Sacral Chakra: Located below the navel, associated with emotions and desires. Meditating on the sacral chakra can help us stimulate inner inspiration and creative thinking.

Recommended Essential Oils and Scents for the Artwork

- Rose: Has a soothing and mood-enhancing effect, helping to stimulate self-love and happiness.

- Sandalwood: Has a calming and soothing effect, helping to enhance inner peace and self-acceptance.

Related Crystals

- Rose Quartz: Helps enhance the energy of the heart chakra, promoting emotional expression and acceptance.

- Yellow Jade: Helps enhance the energy of the sacral chakra, boosting self-worth and inner stability.

Additionally, you can add these small practices daily:

- Creative Writing: Write down your feelings about yourself, including strengths and weaknesses. Then, write a letter to yourself, expressing care and encouragement. This writing approach can help you better understand and accept yourself.

- Body Care: Spend a few minutes each day paying attention to your body, doing simple massages or stretching exercises. Caring for your body can enhance overall happiness and self-love awareness.

- Gratitude Journal: Write down three things you are grateful for every day, whether big or small. This practice can enhance positive emotions and happiness.

Through these steps, you can effectively enhance your ability for self-acceptance and self-love, finding inner peace and harmony.

Creating Time: Self-Acceptance and Self-Love

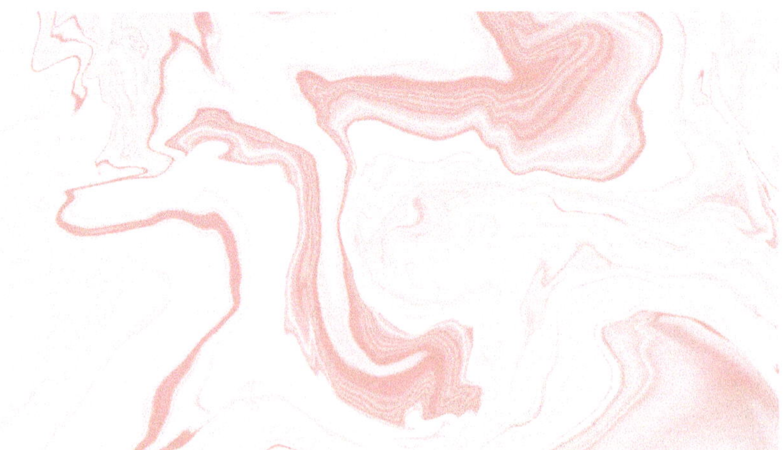

Now, let's review and master multisensory meditation through a comprehensive practice. This exercise is not only a meditation practice but also helps you enhance your self-acceptance and self-love, creating your meditation art.

Steps:

- Prepare Materials: Prepare some modeling clay in various colors.

- Create a Relaxing Space: Following Feng Shui principles, find a corner at home filled with natural light, preferably in the east, as this direction is associated with the energy of renewal and vitality. Ensure the space is clean and tidy, introducing plants or natural elements like flowers and green plants to enhance the space's natural energy.

- Enter Meditation State: Sit in the chosen space, gently close your eyes, take a few deep breaths, and relax all your muscles. Imagine yourself in a warm place, feeling the atmosphere and energy there.

- Start Creating: Open your eyes, sculpt different shapes using the modeling clay in your hands, expressing your emotions and inspirations. These can be abstract forms or specific objects. Focus on your feelings and emotional expressions during the creation process. Don't worry about the outcome; enjoy the process.

- Incorporate Scents: During creation, light rose or sandalwood essential oil lets the scent permeate the space, further enhancing your sensory experience and deepening the meditation effect.

- Use Crystals: During meditation and creation, touch rose quartz and yellow jade, feeling their energy flow, enhancing the depth of meditation and the power of self-acceptance.

- Taste Integration: After meditation and creation, enjoy a cup of passion fruit juice, experiencing the unique taste stimulation and feeling inner peace and joy.

- Conclude and Record Experiences: After completing the modeling clay creation, quietly appreciate your work and record your feelings and experiences. Note the energy changes in the surrounding environment and feel the enhancement of self-acceptance and self-love.

Interactive Questions and Reflections

- How do you practice self-acceptance and self-love in your daily life? What new methods can you try to enhance your ability to love yourself?
- How do you think self-acceptance and self-love help your personal growth and happiness?
- When facing inner challenges and difficulties, how do you use meditation and art creation to enhance your self-acceptance and self-love?

Document your reflections in a personal notebook. Take time to review them. Sharing your thoughts and art creations with the group is highly recommended to enhance the experience.

Meet, share, and grow with creative spirits globally.
(Group QR code is located in p37)

References
- Neff, K. D. (2011). Self-Compassion: Stop Beating Yourself Up and Leave Insecurity Behind.
- Neff, K. D. (2003). Self-Compassion: An Alternative Conceptualization of a Healthy Attitude Toward Oneself.

CHAPTER VII
SPIRITUAL GROWTH

EXPLORATION AND DISCOVERY

Do you know who you are? Do you know what kind of growth path suits you?

> ## The Dao that can be told is not the eternal Dao.
> ### — Dao De Jing, Chapter 1

This wisdom reveals the profound and infinite nature of the Tao. Through spiritual exploration and discovery, we can continuously grow and find peace and contentment within our hearts. This growth is not only about the pursuit of external knowledge but also about the deep understanding of our inner world. Through spiritual exploration, we can discover our potential, improving the quality of our lives and our sense of happiness.

Interpretation and Extension:

"The Tao that can be told is not the eternal Tao" indicates that the true Tao cannot be described in words. It transcends the limits of language and resides deep within our hearts. Spiritual exploration and discovery are about getting closer to this Tao and finding inner peace and harmony. Each person's spiritual growth path is unique, and only through continuous exploration and discovery can we genuinely understand our inner world.

Spiritual exploration is a deepening of self-awareness and a pursuit of the meaning of life. Through meditation, reading, traveling, and self-reflection, we can continuously expand the boundaries of our minds, finding inner peace and harmony.

This exploration not only helps us better understand ourselves but also helps us better understand others and the world.

Spiritual Exploration, Inner Growth, and Self-Discovery

Spiritual exploration can expand our inner boundaries and promote the progress and growth of the soul. Through continuous self-discovery and deep thinking, we can find inner peace and harmony and enhance our ability to cope with life's challenges.

Spiritual exploration is like a journey within, allowing us to understand our emotions, thoughts, and behavioral patterns deeply. We see our inner world more clearly through meditation, writing, and self-reflection, discovering the wisdom and strength hidden within. Brené Brown, in Daring Greatly, points out that facing our vulnerabilities and imperfections can make us stronger and more confident (Brown, 2012).

Inner exploration helps us discover and transcend our limitations. We identify and deal with inner conflicts and contradictions through deep thinking and reflection, gradually achieving self-acceptance and self-love. This self-understanding and acceptance lay a solid foundation for our mental health, enabling us to maintain inner peace and firmness when facing various challenges in life.

Spiritual exploration is not limited to the inner world but includes exploring the external world. Through traveling, reading, and interacting with different people, we broaden our horizons and absorb diverse experiences and perspectives. This external exploration promotes spiritual growth, making us more open, tolerant, and empathetic. As psychologist Martin Seligman points out in his research on positive psychology, positive relationships and prosperous life experiences can significantly enhance our sense of happiness and life satisfaction (Seligman, 2011).

Scientific research shows that meditation can significantly improve mood, reduce stress, and enhance the function of brain regions related to attention, emotional regulation, and spiritual exploration (Kabat-Zinn, 1990). Meditation can clear our minds, focus on the present, and find peace and harmony. Long-term meditation can enhance emotional regulation and improve self-awareness and inner wisdom, further deepening our spiritual exploration.

Multisensory art meditation further deepens our spiritual exploration through multi-layered sensory stimulation. By combining visual, auditory, and tactile experiences, multisensory art meditation helps us perceive and understand our inner world more comprehensively, enhancing focus and emotional regulation and connecting deeply with our inner selves, discovering inner wisdom and strength. It enables us to understand our inner needs and desires more clearly, find inner peace and harmony, and achieve spiritual growth.

Spiritual exploration also helps us find the meaning and purpose of life. Abraham Maslow's theory of self-actualization points out that after meeting basic needs, humans pursue higher-level needs such as belonging, respect, and self-actualization (Maslow, 1943). Through continuous spiritual exploration, we can clarify our values and life goals, finding a direction that truly fulfills us and brings happiness.

In summary, spiritual exploration and meditation are essential to spiritual growth. Through internal and external exploration, we can expand our inner boundaries, discover our potential, and achieve significant progress and development in our souls. This exploration makes us more open, firm, and wise, enabling us to face life's challenges calmly, find inner peace and harmony, and achieve proper spiritual growth and happiness.

My Experience: From Chaos to Clarity - My Journey of Exploration, Spiritual Awakening and Growth

During my studies at RISD, I constantly pondered the brevity of life and how to make the most of it. I often asked myself, what kind of life would be without regrets? Although I pursued my passion for design and artistic creation after graduation, the monotony of my work limited my understanding of other aspects of society. Seeking new possibilities, I left my comfort zone and embarked on a "life diversification" journey.

Leaving the design industry, I established a non-profit cultural organization as an art curator and education summit planner, collaborating with Chinese museums and educational institutions to organize a series of art and cultural exchange activities. Later, I founded an online knowledge-sharing platform called Synking, which significantly impacted my life. We invited alumni from top universities and art schools worldwide to share their insights and perspectives monthly.

This platform was warmly received in China, with over 20,000 people sometimes tuning in to our live broadcasts. We prepared questions carefully and interviewed many outstanding individuals, including renowned professors, top laboratory scientists, bestselling authors, and promising young directors. From them, I saw a broader aspect of life and learned about many perspectives I had never encountered.

Due to the need for entrepreneurship, I learned how to manage and organize teams and find and create new opportunities. During this period, I also taught myself many business-related skills. This external exploration allowed me to break free from the label of an artist and designer, enabling me to view problems from a more macro perspective.

However, the arrival of the pandemic disrupted my plans. I contracted COVID-19, and everything had to slow down. I also ended a long-term relationship during this low point in my life. I remember that winter vividly, feeling extreme pain and torment, but it also became a turning point that shifted my focus from the external world to the internal one. This realization made me understand that our souls still need time to grow and awaken, even with ample information and resources.

Like a traveler who has experienced the vicissitudes of life, I let go of all resentment, depression, and heartbreak and returned to the embrace of art. During that gray period, art became the bridge connecting me to my inner spiritual world. Like a monk, I turned off my phone and spent my days meditating and creating. Art soothed my inner pain, allowing me to gradually hear my inner voice clearly and finally find the direction for my growth.

External experiences broadened my horizons and understanding, but ultimately, art embraced my soul, allowing me to find true peace and awakening.

This journey made me realize that the meaning of life lies in growth and exploration. True awakening comes from the connection of the soul after countless experiences. Only with clarity and awareness can we see everything clearly; otherwise, no amount of experience will be helpful.

Our time in this world is limited, and within this limited time, we need to explore and experience as much as possible, understanding ourselves in the process. We can only get close to pure happiness and joy by reconnecting with our souls.

Spiritual awakening and growth are continuous exploration, discovery, and understanding. We cannot remain rigid in our current knowledge; we must continually break through, try, feel, and connect from within.

82

Multisensory Art Meditation Practice

Please scan the QR to access the artwork for meditation practice.

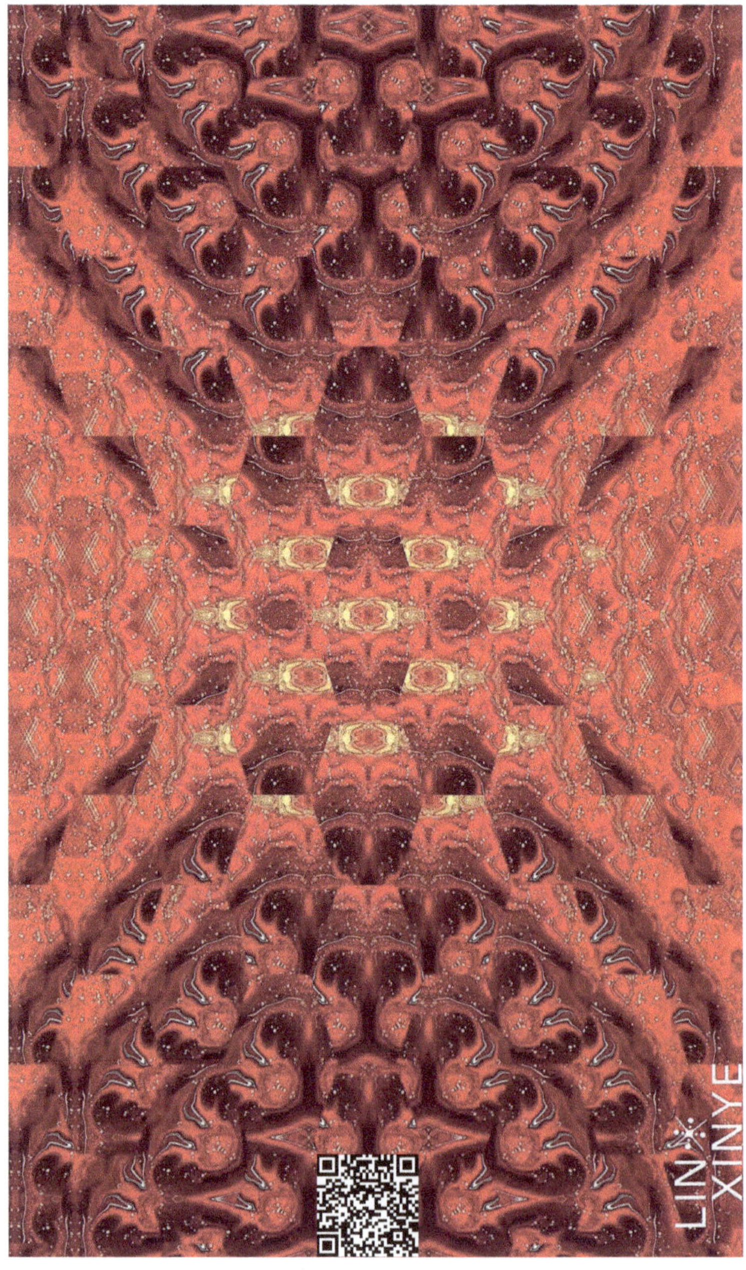

Viewing the artwork in the suggested feng shui direction for a better experience. A projector is recommended to display the artwork on a wall to create a more immersive meditation atmosphere.

Feng Shui Application: Enhancing Energy and Creating a Space for Spiritual Growth

The South symbolizes passion and spirituality. Placing the "Spiritual Growth" artwork in this direction will infuse your meditation process with vibrant energy. Choose a corner filled with natural light, preferably facing south, as this direction is associated with the fire element, bringing enthusiasm and vitality. Keep the space clean and tidy, avoiding clutter, which helps enhance mental clarity and inner peace.

- Body Relaxation Exercises: Before meditation, perform simple yoga or stretching exercises. This will relax every part of your body, prepare you to meditate, and enhance your sensory sensitivity and inner awareness.

- Aromatherapy: While viewing and meditating, light rosemary or chamomile essential oils let the fragrance fill the space, enhancing your sensory experience and meditation effects.

- Crystal Usage: While viewing the artwork and practicing, touch red agate and yellow crystal, feeling their energy flow. This will enhance the depth of your meditation and the power of your spiritual growth.

- Taste Combination: After meditation and creation, enjoy a small bowl of lavender honey tea, experiencing this unique taste stimulation and feeling inner peace and joy.

- Incorporating Natural Elements: Add some natural elements to your meditation space, such as flowers, plants, or stones, touching them to feel their texture and energy, enhancing your connection with nature and promoting inner tranquility and harmony.

- Inspiration Capture: Consider sudden inspirations and ideas during meditation and viewing the artwork. I'd appreciate it if you could record these inspirations and try to apply them in your daily life, exploring their impact on your spiritual growth.

- Color Meditation: After meditation, choose a color that attracts you, close your eyes, imagine being surrounded by this color, and feel the energy and emotional changes it brings, exploring its impact on your soul.

Colors Involved in the Artwork

- Red: Represents energy, strength, and passion, helping to stimulate inner drive and inspiration.

- Gold: Symbolizes spirituality, enlightenment, and wisdom, aiding in enhancing inner peace and harmony.

Chakras Involved in the Artwork

- Heart Chakra: Located at the center of the chest, associated with love and emotions. Meditating on the heart chakra can enhance emotional expression and acceptance.

- Sacral Chakra: Located below the navel, related to emotions and desires. Meditating on the sacral chakra can help stimulate inner inspiration and creativity.

Recommended Essential Oils and Scents for the Artwork

- Rosemary: Has a refreshing and concentration-enhancing effect, helping to improve inner insight and spiritual exploration.

- Chamomile: Has calming and soothing effects, helping to reduce anxiety and enhance inner tranquility.

Related Crystals

- Garnet: Helps enhance the energy of the heart chakra, promoting emotional expression and acceptance.

- Citrine: Helps enhance the energy of the sacral chakra, boosting self-worth and inner stability.

Additionally, you can use these practices to reinforce the effects:

- Daily Meditation: Spend a few minutes daily for simple meditation, focusing on your breath. Through meditation, clear your thoughts and enter a deep inner world, enhancing self-awareness and spiritual growth.

- Spiritual Diary: After viewing the artwork and meditating, pick up a pen and paper and record your feelings and insights from the meditation. Write down your inner dialogues, draw images of your inner world, or create a short poem. Through creative expression, record the results of your spiritual exploration, which will help you better understand and grow.

- Spiritual Sharing Session: After your meditation experience, choose a fixed time each week for a sharing session with friends or family. Everyone can share their feelings and insights from the meditation, encouraging and supporting each other and growing together. This sharing consolidates personal spiritual growth and provides new inspirations and insights from others' experiences.

- Spiritual Art Creation: Schedule a weekly spiritual art creation activity. Based on the insights from your meditation, please feel free to express your spiritual growth and inner exploration. This creation process enhances the spiritual experience and concretizes inner feelings, helping you better understand and grow.

Creating Time: Spiritual Growth Art Creation

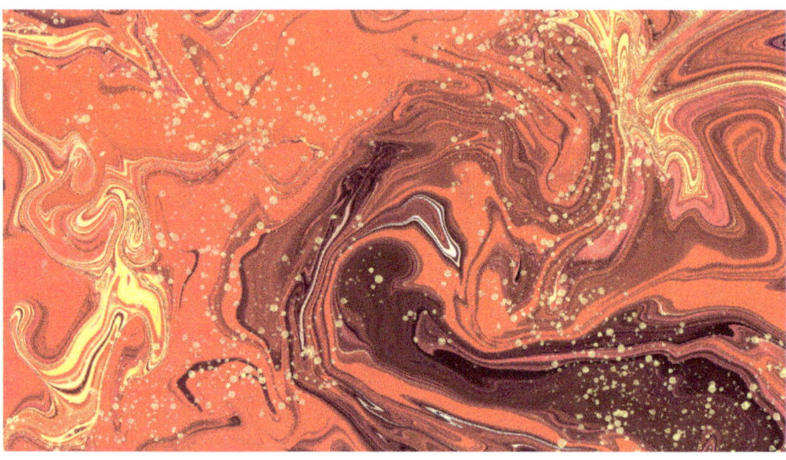

Now, let's practice a comprehensive exercise to master multisensory art meditation. This practice is a form of meditation and helps you enhance your spiritual growth and create your meditation art piece.

Steps:

- Gather Materials: Collect everyday household items such as old magazines, scissors, glue, colored pencils, old fabrics, and paper.

- Create a Relaxing Space: Following Feng Shui principles, find a corner in your home filled with natural light, preferably facing south, as this direction is associated with passion and spirituality. Ensure this space is clean and tidy, and place some plants or natural elements, such as flowers or green plants, to enhance the natural energy of the space.

- Enter a Meditative State: Sit in the chosen space, focus on the "Spiritual Growth" artwork, close your eyes, take a few deep breaths, relax all your muscles, and imagine yourself in a space filled with passion and spirituality, feeling the inner insights and wisdom.

Steps:

- Start Creating: Open your eyes and use the collected materials to create a collage. Cut out images and text from the magazines, combine them with old fabrics and paper, and create artwork expressing your inner feelings and inspiration. During the creation process, focus on your feelings and emotional expression without worrying about the outcome. Enjoy the process.

- Combine with Scent: During the creation process, you can light rosemary or lavender essential oils, letting the scent fill the space, further enhancing your sensory experience and the effects of meditation.

- Use Crystals: Touch red agate and citrine during meditation and creation, feeling their energy flow. This will enhance the depth of your meditation and the power of your spiritual growth.

- Taste Combination: Enjoy a cup of green tea after meditation and creation. The refreshing bitterness helps improve focus and inner peace.

- Conclude and Record Experiences: After completing the collage, quietly appreciate your artwork and record your feelings and experiences. Note the energy changes in the surrounding environment and feel the enhancement of your spiritual growth.

Interactive Questions and Reflections

- How do you practice spiritual growth and exploration in your daily life? What new methods can you try to enhance your spirituality?
- How do you think spiritual growth and exploration help your personal development and sense of happiness?
- How do you use meditation and art creation to enhance your spiritual growth and exploration when facing inner challenges and difficulties?

Document your reflections in a personal notebook. Take time to review them. Sharing your thoughts and art creations with the group is highly recommended to enhance the experience.

Meet, share, and grow with creative spirits globally.
(Group QR code is located in p37)

....

References
- Brown, B. (2012). Daring Greatly: How the Courage to Be Vulnerable Transforms the Way We Live, Love, Parent, and Lead. New York, NY: Gotham Books.
- Seligman, M. E. P. (2011). Flourish: A Visionary New Understanding of Happiness and Well-being. New York, NY: Atria Books.
- Kabat-Zinn, J. (1990). Full Catastrophe Living: Using the Wisdom of Your Body and Mind to Face Stress, Pain, and Illness. New York, NY: Delacorte.
- Maslow, A. H. (1943). A Theory of Human Motivation. Psychological Review, 50(4), 370-396.

CHAPTER VIII
INFINITE POSSIBILITIES

AWAKENING AND TRANSCENDENCE

Thank you for completing this book with me. Although this book is ending, your journey of self-exploration is just beginning. Life is like climbing mountains; the joy of reaching the summit may last only a moment, but most of the time, we are in the process of climbing. The majority of our life consists of these ordinary climbing moments. Learning, living, and relationships are all like this. Experiencing multisensory art and meditation serves as a reminder during the climb, reactivating your senses that may have become numb and allowing you to enjoy the process again. When you learn to enjoy this process, you will gradually awaken and transcend the ordinary.

Plato's Allegory of the Cave in "The Republic" reveals that in our daily lives, we only see the surface of things and overlook the reality behind them. Multisensory art meditation reactivates our senses through direct perception, guiding us to explore and experience the abstract truths hidden behind appearances. When you focus on your inner self, you are like stepping out of the cave, seeing the essence and reality of everything. This awakening is a new understanding of the inner world and a new comprehension of the external world (Plato, 380 BC).

Awakening is an understanding of the inner self and a re-recognition of the external world. Through deep thought and inner exploration, we can find inner strength. This strength helps us maintain inner peace and firmness when facing difficulties.

Building on awakening, we can attempt to break through and transcend ourselves. Through continuous learning and growth, we can break internal constraints and embrace life's infinite possibilities. This is a spiritual sublimation and a comprehensive enhancement of life. Transcendence is the discovery of inner strength and the exploration of the external world. We can broaden our horizons and cognition by continuously learning and trying new things, thus achieving self-transcendence.

This transcendence allows us to better understand ourselves and others and enables us to better understand the world, maintaining inner peace and firmness when facing various life challenges.

Friedrich Nietzsche mentioned in "Thus Spoke Zarathustra" that "One must still have chaos in oneself to be able to give birth to a dancing star." This sentence once inspired me, and I want to share it with you. I hope it can give you the strength to challenge and breakthrough continually. Through meditation and multisensory art creation, you can gain inner inspiration and bravely step toward infinite possibilities (Nietzsche, 1883).

You are not alone on this journey of exploration and growth. I am on this path with you. Let us explore and learn together, becoming the versions of ourselves we most admire. The insights and shares of multisensory art meditation I have summarized can light up your life and awaken your senses. May you be inspired on this journey, find inner peace and happiness, and experience a more wonderful and fascinating world.

Practical Applications and Future Outlook

Even though this book's journey is ending, you can always revisit it when needed.

Suggestions and Tips for Practice:

- Set Daily Meditation Goals: Spend at least 15 minutes each day meditating. You can follow the meditation methods in this book or any preferred meditation style. Set a fixed time and place to develop the habit. This will become a spiritual pillar in your daily life, helping you maintain inner peace and harmony.

- Find a Support Community: Find or create a support group to share your experiences and gains with others and receive support and encouragement. You can also join some online communities where we can exchange insights and grow together.

- Record Your Growth Insights: Keep a growth journal to record each reflection's experiences and insights. This is a review and summary of yourself and a guide for the future, helping you better understand and reflect on yourself.

- Combine Creative Expression: After meditation, continue expressing yourself creatively through writing, drawing, or other art forms. Let your creativity be fully unleashed in the exploration and find your true self.

- Set Long-Term Goals: Set some long-term goals for your journey of self-improvement to maintain motivation and direction. Achieving each small goal is a big step toward spiritual growth, helping you continue to make progress.

- Join the Community: Join the Artful Awakening group to connect with creative spirits, share your experiences, and grow together. Scan the QR code to find the discussion group for Artful Awakening and meet creative spirits worldwide.

Connect, get inspired, and grow with other creative spirits.

linxinye.com/group/artful-awakening/
Scan the QR code to learn more

Gratitude and Blessings

Thank you for completing this book with me. Throughout this journey, I hope you have felt the power of art meditation and are willing to continue on this path. Use art meditation to light up your life, open new chapters, find inner peace and happiness, and achieve spiritual growth. May each of us live out the version of ourselves we admire, using art and meditation to create a more beautiful and harmonious world.

I will continue to share more about my multisensory art and meditation journey, accompanying you in exploring the world of multisensory art and meditation.

If you want more inspiration and guidance, please subscribe to my newsletter on my website, www.linxinye.com, and follow my Instagram account @ _linxinye
Feel free to leave comments; we can exchange insights and share experiences, progressing together on this path of exploration and growth.

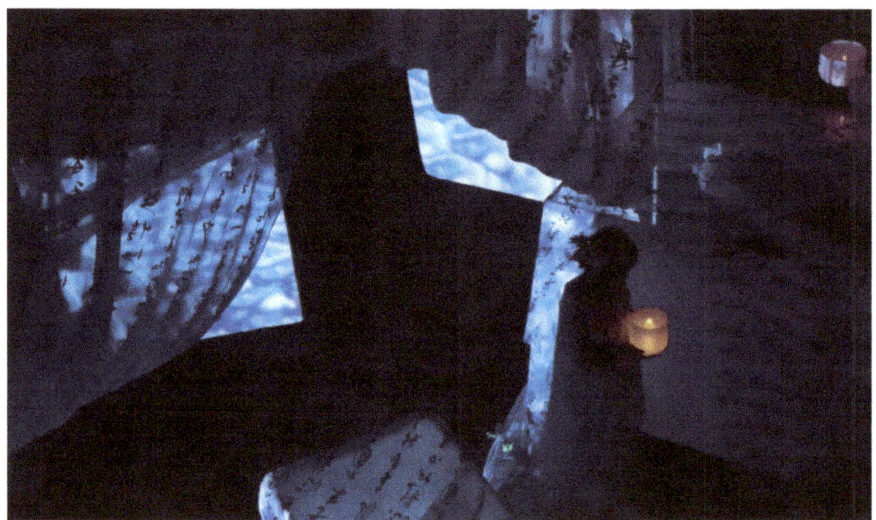

Floating Dream -Live Immersive & Interactive Art Performance and Solo Exhibition, San Francisco, 2023

A New Project Invitation

As I wrote this book, I gradually realized that my creations are not merely expressions of myself but also bridges to connect with those who truly need art to soothe their souls and convey strength. Therefore, I have decided to launch a new project called "One Hundred Blessings"

The goal of "One Hundred Blessings" is to convey energy and blessings through art. I hope to bring the healing power of art to those who need it most.

Art is not just about creation; it is a bridge that can connect hearts, heal wounds, and spread love and hope.

I sincerely invite you to share your stories with me. Whether they are moments of joy or challenges in life, your experiences can become sources of inspiration for my creations. Your stories will help me infuse this project with even more emotion and strength, allowing art to illuminate the lives of more people.

Please write email to me (xinyelin@linxinye.com) and share your stories, so we can witness together how the power of art can touch hearts and heal the world. I look forward to your letters and hope to send you a unique blessing in my future creations.

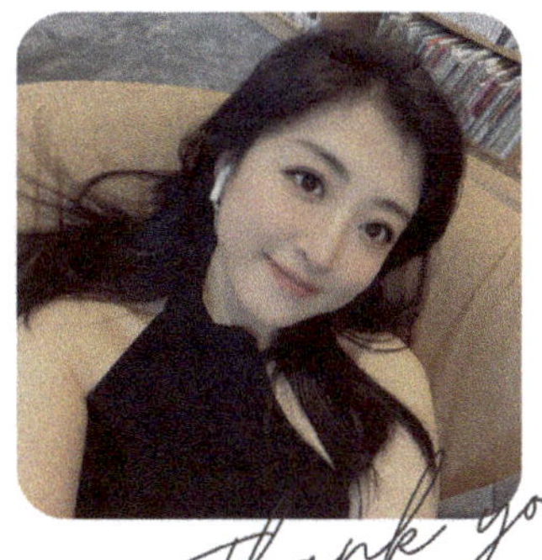

Create, Reflect, Transcend

www.linxinye.com